S0-ADH-530

WITHDRAWN FROM LIBRARY

MONTGOMERY COLLEGE LIBRARY
ROCKVILLE CAMPUS

ESSAYS
MORAL AND POLITE

ESSAYS
MORAL AND
POLITE
1660-1714

Selected and Edited by
**JOHN AND CONSTANCE
MASEFIELD**

Essay Index Reprint Series

BOOKS FOR LIBRARIES PRESS
FREEPORT, NEW YORK

PR
1365
M3   R 72   4549
1971

INTERNATIONAL STANDARD BOOK NUMBER:
0-8369-2243-3

LIBRARY OF CONGRESS CATALOG CARD NUMBER:
78-157966

PRINTED IN THE UNITED STATES OF AMERICA

ROUGHLY speaking, the authors included in this volume flourished between the Restoration and the death of Queen Anne. The fifty-four years may be divided into two periods, of which the first was dominated by the Court-party, the Earl of Rochester, the Earl of Roscommon, and Sir Charles Sedley; and the second by Addison and Steele, and the greater genius of Dean Swift. The age as a whole was a critical age. During the earlier period the human intellect took stock of its past achievements, and determined for itself certain rules very proper for things stationary. There was never an age in which intellectual matters were more highly prized. Nor has there ever been an age more certain of its own surpassing merit, on grounds more slender. Soon after the Revolution, however, the criticism that had been directed on Chaucer, Shakespeare, and Milton, and in personal attack, was turned on the depravities and flippancies of polite society. This change of attitude was due, as far as

such a change can be due to the influence of
one man, to the righteous invective of Jeremy
Collier.   The essayists who followed him
maintained his high motive, though their
prose was as elegant as the verse of the
poets of Charles's court, and though they
still adhered to the French rules for drama,
which these poets had introduced.

It was not a creative age; for the creative
age had ended in the confusion of the civil wars,
and in the large utterance of the Protectorate.
With the Restoration had come excess, and
consequent disease.   With the Revolution
began a more salutary course—a course, as
it were, of physic, and rule-of-life—to enable
the debauched intellect to recover its ancient
strength of nerve.   The rules it imposed upon
itself were rules only proper to conditions of
the kind.   To a literary society, inspired only
by the grossest of physical appetites, the
dictum that

'Want of decency is want of sense,'

is at once purgative and wholesome.   To a
literary society, drawing frankly and sanely
from the whole of life, such a statement would
be useless, as implying an absurd limitation.
It is one thing to stamp a Tom D'Urfey, or

an Earl of Rochester, into his merited sewer,
but quite another to order Juliet's Nurse into
the kitchen, and Mercutio to a sporting club.
Again, a literary society, brought up, not
upon life, and the pageants and stress of
life, like the Elizabethans, but upon ancient
authors, and rules deduced from those authors,
is qualified only for the appreciation of itself,
and of things like itself. It condemns things
unlike itself, for their unlikeness, as sparrows
attack escaped canaries.

By the time of the Revolution, the duties
of writers, and the decencies of writing, had
been defined with such authority that much
of Chaucer, of Shakespeare, and of Milton
had been re-written by those in favour of
the new rules. All earlier English writing,
which, from its breadth and fervour, failed to
conform to these standards, was disparaged
as incorrect. The subject-matter, the material of authors, which, in the past, had been
man's passion, or hope, however rude or wild,
was then forced to an unwilling conformity
with the amended manner. Character, in
the drama of the period, was made to show
itself polite, rather than human. The heroic
person, in contemporary tragedy, showed

himself, not as say Coriolanus showed himself, by noble action, but by the speaking of fine sentiments in a fine attitude. A man wrote of an event, not as it had happened, from the passions of humanity, but as he thought it ought to have happened, had Providence learned the unities before tampering with red clay.

But while the dramatist, in his tawdry trappings, kept ponderously aloof from all reality, the essayists, working in a medium proper to the time, not borrowed from a time wholly alien in temper, were able to approach life freshly, and to judge it, if not profoundly, at least with delicate art. They do not give us great literature, but they give us much that is charming, and wholesome, and whimsical, in very dainty and careful English. They have not the passion of the Elizabethans, nor the moral grandeur of the men of the Protectorate. Their strength had been sapped by the fiat that certain things which might offend certain readers had better be ignored. We find them bent on reforming, not the world, but their literary manners, and some of the drawing-rooms which they frequented.

Their care for the manner, for the clothing of the thought, reduced poetry to exact mechanics, making a poem little more than regulated, antithetical prose. But while it fettered poetry (which demands freedom) it also fettered prose, and reduced wildness, and rhetoric, and poetical rhapsody, to order, and measure, and balance, and exact law. In the reign of Elizabeth, when prose had been artificial, as with Lyly, or braggart and wild as with Nash and Dekker, our writers produced sentences such as—

'Why should I go gadding and firgigging after firking flantado amfibologies? wit is wit, and good will is good will.'

Or

'For thy flaring frounzed Periwigs low dangled down with lovelocks, shalt thou have thy head side dangled down with more Snakes than ever it had hayres.'

Or

'Pan is a god, Apollo is no more. Comparisons cannot be odious, where the deities are equall. This pipe (my sweet pipe) was once a nymph, a faire nymph, once my lovely mistresse, now my heavenly musique. Tell mee, Apollo, is there any instrument so sweet to play on as one's mistresse? Had thy lute been of lawrell, and the strings of Daphne's haire, thy tunes might have beene compared to thy notes; for then Daphne would have added to thy stroke sweetnesse, and to thy thoughts melodie.'

Two generations later, when prose was gorgeous and solemn, like great poetry, we find passages such as—

'Others, rather than be lost in the uncomfortable night of nothing, were content to recede into the common being, and make one particle of the public soul of all things, which was no more than to return into their unknown and divine original again. Egyptian ingenuity was more unsatisfied, contriving their bodies in sweet consistencies, to attend the return of their souls. But all was vanity, feeding the wind, and folly. The Egyptian mummies, which Cambyses or time hath spared, avarice now consumeth. Mummy is become merchandize, Mizraim cures wounds, and Pharaoh is sold for balsam.'

Or

'Behold now this vast city: a city of refuge, the mansion house of liberty, en-

compast and surrounded with his protection:
the shop of warre hath not there more anvils
and hammers waking, to fashion out the
plates and instruments of armed justice in
defence of beleaguered truth, than there be
pens and heads there, sitting by their
studious lamps, musing, searching, revolving
new motions and ideas wherewith to present
as with their homage and their fealty the
approaching Reformation, others as fast
reading, trying all things, assenting to the
force of reason and convincement.'

But with the coming of the new rules,
such prose, whether wild or noble, became
impossible. Instead of the splendid music
of the prose of Milton, or of Jeremy Taylor,
or of Sir Thomas Browne, or of Thomas
Fuller, we have the calm, sedate, and
ordered rhythms of writers schooled in a
new tradition. We have but to turn to
Dryden's Preface to 'All for Love,' to note
the difference; and to see how clearly and
coldly and decorously the new writers make
their statements.

'All reasonable men have long since concluded, that the hero of the poem ought not
to be a character of perfect virtue, for then

he could not, without injustice, be made
unhappy; nor yet altogether wicked, because
he could not then be pitied. I have therefore steered the middle course; and have
drawn the character of Antony as favourably
as Plutarch, Appian, and Dion Cassius would
give me leave: the like I have observed in
Cleopatra. That which is wanting to work
up the pity to a greater height, was not
afforded me by the story.'

Setting aside the work of Bishop Berkeley,
and the satire of Swift, it may be said that
the work of these writers, even at its best,
as in the charming essays of Addison, and
the lucid exposition of Dryden, is not great
work. It has been said that the art of a
man cannot exceed his culture; and the
culture of the time means little more than
a knowledge of Latin, and of some French
essays. The writers are all clever, and
brilliant, and accomplished, but we leave
their writings with the feeling that they
lived in an unpleasant age, and that their
lives, amid all the gilt, and pretence, and
elaborate and squalid finery, were not the
lives of great men. They were less than
their work. If we remember them at all,

as apart from their work, we remember them
by their quarrels, and their personal failings,
or by the bitter words others have spoken of
them. It is not thus that we think of Keats,
or Milton, or Chaucer.

In this little book we have gathered together a number of prose writings by various
hands. The selection is not by any means
representative, for we have been forced to
omit several writers (such as Sir William
Temple, William Penn, Robert Barclay, and
Dean Swift) owing to the length of the pieces
we wished to include. The selections from
Jeremy Collier, and from Steele, have been
taken from their less familiar works. We
have given specimens of nearly every kind
of prose writing for which the age is famed.
In Jeremy Collier you have the militant
moralist; in Dryden and Shaftesbury the
critic; in Cowley and Evelyn the leisured
trifler. L'Estrange represents the translator,
while Bishop Berkeley represents philosophy.
Steele and Addison, the mirthful and tender
comrades, are more various than their fellows,
as the line of Juvenal, which they so often
quoted, would suggest.

J. and C. M.

JOHN EVELYN

THE PREFACE

From Mundus Muliebris, or The Ladies'
Dressing Room Unlocked, and her
Toilette Spread.

This Paper was not to come abroad without
a preface as well as comment, for instruction
of our young master, who, newly launched
from the University (where he has lost a year
or two), is not yet travelled, or, if haply he has
made 'le petit tour' (with the formal Thing
his Governor), having never yet read Tully's
'Offices' through; since he came from school,
sets up for a beau, and equipped for the town
at his return, comes to seek adventures in an
ocean full of rocks, and shelves, and wants a
skilful pilot to steer him, as much as any
vessel that goes to the Indies; and oftentimes
returns home leaky, and as poorly freighted,
as those who have been near shipwrecked, or
lost their voyage.

It is for direction of such as are setting out
towards this great and famous emporium
(whether the design be for miss or marriage)
what cargo he must provide; not as mer-

A   I

chants do for America, glass beads and
baubles in exchange for gold and pearl; but
gold and pearl, and all that's precious, for
that which is of less value than knives and
children's rattles.

You see, squires, what you are to prepare
for as adventurers, or by way of barter, if
you think to traffic here, and to carry the
fair one, especially if she be at her own disposal or (being come some considerable time
out of the country) has been initiated into the
conversation of the town. The refined lady
expects her servants and humble admirers
should court her in the forms and decencies of
making love in fashion. In order to this, you
must often treat her at the play, the park, and
the music; present her at the raffle, follow her
to Tunbridge at the season of drinking of
waters, though you have no need of them
yourself. You must improve all occasions of
celebrating her shape, and how well the mode
becomes her, though it be ne'er so fantastical
and ridiculous; and she sings like an angel,
dances like a goddess; and that you are
charmed with her wit and beauty. Above
all, you must be sure to find some fault or
imperfection in all other ladies of the town,
and to laugh at the fops like yourself. With
this, a little practice will qualify you for the
conversation and mystery of the Ruelle; and
if the whole morning be spent between the
glass and the comb, that your perruque sit

well, and cravat-strings be adjusted as things
of importance ; with these and the like accomplishments you will emerge a consummate
beau —— Anglice, a coxcomb. But the dancing master will still be necessary to preserve
your good mien, and fit you for the winter-
ball.

Thus you see, young Sparks, how the style
and method of wooing is quite changed as
well as the language, since the days of our
forefathers (of unhappy memory, simple and
plain men as they were) who courted and
chose their wives for their modesty, frugality,
keeping at home, good housewifery, and
other economical virtues then in reputation.
And when the young damsels were taught all
these in the country and their parents' houses,
the portion they brought was more in virtue
than money, and she was a richer match than
one who could have brought a million, and
nothing else to commend her. The presents
which were made when all was concluded,
were a ring, a necklace of pearl, and perhaps
another fair jewel, the ' Bona Paraphernalia '
of her prudent mother, whose nuptial kirtle,
gown, and petticoat, lasted as many anniver-
saries as the happy couple lived together, and
were at last bequeathed with a purse of old
gold, rose-nobles, spur-royals, and spankers,
as an house-loom to her grand-daughter.

They had cupboards of ancient, useful
plate, whole chests of damask for the table,

and store of fine holland sheets (white as the
driven snow) and fragrant of rose and lavender
for the bed ; and the sturdy oaken bedstead
and furniture of the house, lasted one whole
century ; the shovel-board, and other long
tables both in hall and parlour, were as fixed
as the freehold ; nothing was movable save
joint-stools, the black jacks, silver tankards,
and bowls. And though many things fell out
between the cup and the lip, when nappy ale,
March beer, Metheglin, Malmsey, and old
Sherry, got the ascendant amongst the Blue-
Coats and Badges, they sung 'Old Symon,'
and 'Cheviot Chase,' and danced brave
'Arthur,' and were able to draw a bow, that
made the proud Monsieur tremble at the
whizze of the grey goose feather. It was
then ancient hospitality was kept up in
town and country, by which the tenants were
enabled to pay their landlords at punctual
day. The poor were relieved bountifully, and
charity was as warm as the kitchen, where
the fire was perpetual.

In those happy days, Sure-Foot, the grave
and steady mare, carried the good knight and
his courteous lady behind him to church, and
to visit the neighbourhood, without so many
hell-carts, rattling coaches, and a crew of
damme-lacqueys, which a grave livery servant
or two supplied, who rode before and made
way for his Worship.

Things of use were natural, plain, and

4

wholesome ; nothing was superfluous, nothing
necessary wanting ; and men of estate studied
the public good, and gave example of true
piety, loyalty, justice, sobriety, charity, and
the good neighbourhood composed most
differences. Perjury, suborning witnesses,
alimony, avowed adulteries, and misses
(publicly owned) were prodigies in those days,
and laws were reason, not craft, when men's
titles were secure, and they served their
generation with honour ; left their patrimonial
estates improved to an hopeful heir, who,
passing from the free school to the college,
and thence to the Inns of Court, acquainting
himself with a competent tincture of the laws
of his country, followed the example of his
worthy ancestors ; and if he travelled abroad,
it was not to count steeples, and bring home
feather and ribbon, and the sins of other
nations ; but to gain such experience as
rendered him useful to his prince and country
upon occasion, and confirmed him in the love
of both of them above any other.

The virgins and young ladies of that golden
age (quaesierunt lanam et linum) put their
hands to the spindle, nor disdained they the
needle ; were obsequious, and helpful to their
parents ; instructed in the managing of the
family, and gave presages of making excellent wives ; nor then did they read so many
romances, see so many plays and farces, set
up for visits, and have their days of audience,

5

and idle pastime. Honest gleek, ruff, and honours, diverted the ladies at Christmas, and they knew not so much as the names of ombre, comet, and basset. Their retirements were devout and religious books, and their recreations in the distillatory, the knowledge of plants and their virtues, for the comfort of their poor neighbours, and use of the family, which wholesome plain diet, and kitchen physic, preserved in perfect health. In those days, the scurvy, spleen, etc., were scarce heard of, till foreign drinks and mixtures were wantonly introduced. Nor were the young gentlewomen so universally afflicted with hysterical fits; nor, though extremely modest, at all melancholy, or less gay, and in good humour; they could touch the lute and virginal, sing like to the Damask Rose—and their breath was as sweet as their voices. They danced the Canarys, Spanish Pavan, and Sellenger's Round upon Sippits, with as much grace and loveliness, as any Isaac, Monsieur, or Italian of them all can teach with his top-call and apish postures.

To show you then, how the world is alter'd among us, since foreign manners, the luxury, (more than Asiatic, which was the final ruin of the greatest, wisest, and most noble monarchy upon earth) has universally obtained among us, corrupting ancient simplicity; and in what extravagant form the young gallant we described is to court the Sex, and make his address (whether his expedition be for marriage or mistress) it has been thought good by some charitable hands, to present him with an enumeration of particulars, and computation of the charges of the adventurer.

JEREMY COLLIER

AN ESSAY UPON GAMING
IN A DIALOGUE

Callimachus.—I don't like your arguing so
much for the sovereignty of *chance*: I wish
you have not been dipping in Epicurus's
philosophy box, if you should fancy the world
no better than a carnal rencounter of atoms,
there is no need of confuting this hypothesis.
You have confessed already, their mystery
and tricking in your management. Now this
is enough to disable the application, and spoil
your parallel.

Dolomedes.—I 'll not try to think so if I can
help it. Most people are kind to themselves,
neither do I intend to be out of the fashion.
And to justify our liberty somewhat further,
you may please to observe there 's a great deal
of danger in our employment. A man may
safer make a voyage to the East Indies, or
take service in the field, than set up for a
gamester. Our profession is a state of War,
though we are not always in action. When
the loss goes deep, and especially, when our
art happens to be discovered, we sometimes

8

draw a quarrel upon us ; thus we are forced to fight in defence of our plunder. And when a man takes his meat off his sword's point, 'twould be hard to grudge him the relish on 't.

Callimachus.—If some gentlemen, who risk it no less than you do, should offer this plea at the Old Bailey, I 'm afraid they 'd make little on 't. Bravery upon the road, and venturing a chance for a man's life, is counted no great recommendation of that business. But to come closer to the matter, gaming is commonly scandalous in the motive, foul in the management, and frightful in the consequence. Part of this charge you have confessed already, and the rest I 'm ready to make good.

Dolomedes.—For once I 'd undergo the penance to hear you. By knowing the worst of the case, I may probably recollect myself to advantage, and be better prepared for defence.

Callimachus.—To begin then ; 'Tis Covetousness which generally leads to this diversion, as you call it. If you observe, when people play nothing, they are unusually negligent and heavy; good luck can't keep them from growing weary: they almost sleep through the amusement, and victory brings little satisfaction. But when there 's money in the articles, why loss and gain has a weight upon the fancy: this is a strange awakening consideration. Now there 's a new

9

air of liveliness and concern; their looks and
motion discover business and application;
there's more vigour and guard in their conduct, and they play upon the stretch of their
understanding. And what can be the meaning of these different appearances? Is it not
the prospect of the prize, and the hopes of
sweeping the board? If their aim was only
to secure themselves, and come off without
damage, they'd scarcely risk a considerable
interest, and put it to the venture whether the
money in their pocket should be their own. I
grant over-reigning bashfulness, want of
courage, and mistaken notions of breeding,
may possibly surprise young people, and carry
them beyond their humour, but when they
are once bitten they'll grow more hardy and
discerning, and choose rather to look a little
singular, than be sociable at so high an
expense; for unless inclination draws, people
seldom go deep out of ceremony and compliance.

'Tis plain therefore, where gain has so much
the ascendant, covetousness is at the bottom.
Now this vice has a craving appetite, and is
never satisfied, neither is it anywhere more
scandalously visible than in the business
before us. Your gamester is extremely lean
in his principle: he hopes to trade upon the
most unreasonable terms imaginable, and to
carry off a man's property, without giving
anything in exchange. This is the case,

unless you 'll take his company for an equiva-
lent, or the fatigue of ill-luck for a valuable
consideration.   To be clear, when I play with
you for a sum, I tell you in effect, I 'll do my
best to spoil your diversion, to send you home
with your head disturbed, your pocket light,
and your heart heavy.   And is there not a
great deal of friendship and generosity in this
profession?

Dolomedes.—Did not I tell you ours is a sort
of military business?   Play is fighting for
money and dominion.   I say for dominion, for
empire is commonly extended in proportion to
the purse ;—the more you have the farther you
may command.   And since both parties are
upon terms of hostility, since we stand the
hazard of the contest, why should we let any
serviceable capacity lie idle?   Why should
we baulk our good fortune, in compliance to
the satisfaction of those we engage with?
What General stops the course of his victory,
only for fear of making the enemy melancholy,
and putting him out of humour, for being
well-beaten? If they distrust their preparation,
if they suspect a superiority against them ; if
they want skill to discover a stratagem, why
have they not the wit to be quiet, and keep out
of harm's way?   They know 'tis not in our
power to force a battle.   I confess 'tis not
unusual to see a bubble sufficiently mortified ;
but we must get our living ; compassion won't
subsist us ; we meet with little tenderness

ourselves. And besides, if people will venture a grating disappointment, and raise the vapour from their own folly, they must take it for their pains.

Callimachus.—That may be the farthest of your concern. But I can't help observing that playing deep sets the spirits on float, strikes the mind strongly into the face, and discovers a man's weakness very remarkably. Cards and dice, etc., command the humour no less than the moon does the tide; you may see the passions come up with the dice, and ebb and flow with the fortune of the game; what alternate returns of hope and fear, of pleasure and regret, are frequently visible upon such occasions? As you say gaming is an image of war; the sudden turns of success are easily discernible; the advances of victory, or ill-luck, make a strange revolution in the blood. The countenance takes its tincture from the chance, and appears in the colours of the prospect. With what anxiousness is the issue expected? You would think a jury of life and death was gone out upon them. The sentence for execution is not received with more concern than the unlucky appearance of a cast or card. Thus some people are miserably ruffled, and thrown off the hinges; they seem distressed to an agony; you'd pity them for the meanness of their behaviour; others are no less foolishly pleased; break out with childish satisfaction,

and bring the covetousness of their humour
too much into view.

Now, since play is thus arbitrary over the
passions, who would resign the repose of his
mind, and the credit of his temper, to the
mercy of chance? Who would stake his
discretion upon such unnecessary hazards?
And throw the dice, whether he should be
in his wits or not?

Dolomedes.—This does not always follow.
Some people play without the least offensive-
ness or ruffle; and lose great sums, very
great, with all the decency and indifference
imaginable. And when a man bears up thus
handsomely against misfortune; when that,
which crushes another, is not felt upon his
shoulders; when all this force and firmness
is found within himself, must it not be a
pleasing discovery?

Callimachus.—Alas . . . this insensibleness
is rarely met with. Very few are proof
against a shrewd chance to this degree.
When misfortune strikes home, 'tis seldom
decently received; their temper goes off with
their money. For, according to the proverb,
' Qui perd le sien, perd le sens.' And here one
loss usually makes people desperate. and
leads to another. And now the gentlemen
of your function are extremely vigilant to
improve the opportunity, and observe the
current of the passions. You know very
well when a man's head grows misty with

ill-luck; when the spleen comes over his understanding, and he has fretted himself off his guard, he is much the easier conquest. Thus, when your bubbles are going down the hill, you manage accordingly, lend them a push, though their bones are broken at the bottom. But I forgot myself; there's neither mercy nor justice in some people's business.

To return, you know I may take it for granted that your gaming sparks are horribly ruffled when things with a promising face sicken, and sink on the sudden; when they are surprisingly cross-bitten, and success is snatched from their grasp; when this happens, which is not unfrequent, the spirits are up immediately, and they are a storm at the first blast. The train takes fire, and they kindle and flash at the touch, like gunpowder. And when the passions are thus rampant, nothing is more common than oaths, and execrable language: when, instead of blaming their own rashness, and disciplining their folly, they are cursing their stars, and raging against their fate.

These paroxysms of madness run sometimes so high, that you would think the devil had seized the organs of speech, and that they were possessed in every syllable. And to finish farther, these hideous sallies are sometimes carried on to quarrelling and murder. The dice, it may be, are snatched

14

too quick, the cast is disputed, the loading
and legerdemain is discovered :—

'Jamque faces et saxa volant.'

Upon this they run to arms, and after some
artillery discharged in swearing, come to a
close encounter. And thus one of them is
run through the lungs, and left agonising
upon the place. Or, as it happened not long
since (to a tobacconist in London) the
gamester is knocked down with a pint-pot,
and his skull broken: he is forced to be
trepann'd, and then relapsing into play and
drinking, dies of a frenzy.

As to the hazards, they are frightful, and
sufficient to overset the temper of better
principled people than gamesters commonly
are. Have we not heard of ladies losing
hundreds of guineas at a sitting ? And
others, more slenderly stocked, disfurnish
their husband's studies, and play off the
books, which, it may be, helped to feed them.
And when the women are thus courageous,
the men conclude their own sex calls for
a bolder liberty : That they ought to go
farther in danger, and appear more brave in
the methods of ruin. Thus a manor has been
lost in an afternoon, the suit and service
follows the cast, and the right is transferred
sooner than the lawyer can draw the con-
veyance. A box and dice are terrible artillery,
a battery of cannon scarcely plays with more

execution. They make a breach in a castle, and command a surrender in a little time.

The wealth which has been gotten with great industry and hazard, preserved with no less conduct, and growing, it may be, for several ages, is all swept away on the sudden. A fire, or an inundation, can't undo a man with more expedition. If a main battle had been lost, and the enemy had over-run the country, the ravage could hardly have been sooner (i.e. more sharply) felt.

And now, Dolomedes, to wind up the conference :—If humane understandings have any ground to work on ; if the distinctions of good and evil are not purely imaginary; if revelation is more than a romance, how dangerous a business must that of a gamester be ? How frightful will the account of an after reckoning be swell'd ! What loading articles, what complication of guilt, must he expect to be charged with ? 'Tis true, he 'll find the weight of personal misbehaviour enough to sink him ; but this is not all. The contagion of the example, the soliciting a foul cause will make part of the inquiry another day : debauching himself, surprising other people's fortunes, or throwing away his own, does not take in the whole accusation. The proselyting to licentious excesses, the leading on to madness and murder, and all the wickedness consequent to this diversion, must be answered for.

Thus I have briefly reported the case without straining, or unreasonable aggravation. Common-sense will suggest the substance, and matter of fact abundantly justify all that has been said upon this subject. If the business looks black I can't help that; 'tis nature, and not the pencil, which lays on the complexion.

FROM A LETTER TO A LADY, CONCERNING THE NEW PLAY-HOUSE

Perhaps it will be said, that this censure of plays is too harsh and severe; that the true design of them is to commend virtue and to expose vice; so that they may rather be reckoned profitable than hurtful; there being, without doubt, in that great variety of tempers that men are of, some persons that would sooner be laughed out of their vices, than dissuaded from them by graver discourse.

If this was indeed the design of all plays, and if this design was always well prosecuted, much more might be said for going to see plays than can be now; and, for my own part, I should be so far from being an enemy to them, that I should rather advise such persons as your Ladyship is—such, I mean, as are of plentiful fortunes, and have much time lying upon their hands—to spend

B   17

now and then an hour or two in the doing
what might be at the same time both diverting and profitable. But when we are to give
a short judgment concerning anything in
general, which, as it may be circumstantiated,
may be sometimes innocent, and sometimes
bad, we must consider the thing as it generally and for the most part is; and then, I
say — and 'tis what I believe they that have
seen or read most of the plays of our time
must own—that for the generality they seem
rather as if they were written with a quite
contrary design; I mean, as if they were
designed to expose and ridicule virtue, and
to make vice appear glorious and praise-
worthy. I must own, madam, that I am
not so competent a judge of this as some
others may be, nor perhaps as your ladyship
is; for I never in my life saw a play, and
have not read very many—a few of them
were sufficient to give me a surfeit, and I
never cared for them since—but so far as I
can make a judgment from those which I
have read (and I'm sure I never chose to
read the worst), their design is as wicked
as their composure. For who, and what is
he that in our modern plays is commonly
shown as a pattern to be imitated, the hero
of the play, or the accomplished gentleman?
What is he, I say, for the most part, but
some accomplished debauchee, that regards
neither God nor man, who's above the dis-

cipline of priestcraft, and can commit all
manner of wickedness with a born grace?
Or, if he be not quite so bad as this, yet
his greatest accomplishments usually are,
that he's well skilled in fashions and court-
ships and the humours of the town. This
is the man that is usually shown to the spectators as one whose example 'tis fit all the
young nobility and gentry should conform
themselves to; and I'm sure they do it
too much. And on the other side, what's
he that from one end of the play to the other
is represented as very silly and ridiculous
beyond all the rest of mankind? Is it not
commonly one that has more religion and
more conscience than the rest? One that
has not yet worn off all the impressions of
a good and sober education? One that
can't swear cleverly, nor damn roundly,
nor sin impudently? Who, therefore, as
often as his turn comes to appear upon the
stage, is jested upon, and laughed at, by all
the rest, as superstitious, as priest-ridden, or
as a Puritan and Precisian, or, at best, as
one that has been coarsely and countrily
bred? I have not, I confess, so much minded
the women's characters; your ladyship, I
suppose, may have done that better; but in
those plays which I have happened to read,
very few women have ever been brought
upon the stage but under the notion of jilts,
or such as were easy to be wrought upon.

Which respect commonly given by the play-makers to the fair sex should, methinks, work in the ladies some resentment; it should, methinks, somewhat abate of their forwardness to go to see themselves abused. I'm confident the part of a truly virtuous and religious woman is very rarely acted upon the stage, or if it be, that 'tis very untowardly represented. Tell me, madam, if you can, in what play the character of any such lady is set off with commendation? In what play is it mentioned to the honour of the lady spoken of, that she does spend a good part of every day in her closet, and of many days in the church; that she instructs (her children) in the Catechism, and teaches them to say their prayers; that she looks well to the affairs of her house, and keeps good order in her family; that she is helpful to her afflicted neighbours, just to tradesmen and shopkeepers, and bountiful to the poor; that she is faithful and obedient to her own husband? etc. Nay, tell me, madam (for I should be glad to hear it, and I don't remember that in the plays I have read I have observed it), where in any of our modern plays religion itself is well spoken of, or treated with decent respect? Where any text of Scripture is ever cited or alluded to but in burlesque and abuse? Where the name of God is ever mentioned but in profaneness? Where a minister

is ever brought upon the stage but to be
abused and laughed at? In a word, tell me
the play, that if it was well purged of all
its profaneness, irreligion, and obscenity,
would not have its whole plot almost spoiled
thereby, and be rendered very dull and heavy,
and uninteresting to the spectators? I do
not affirm that there is not so much as one
such play, but I am confident there are but
few such commonly acted. Is it likely, then,
that such plays as are acted for the most part,
and with the greatest applause, should help
to reform the world? Is it not more likely
that they should, and is it not very plain by
experience that they do, help very much to
debauch and corrupt it?

ABRAHAM COWLEY

OF AGRICULTURE

The first wish of Virgil (as you will find anon by his verses) was to be a good philosopher; the second, a good husbandman: and God (whom he seemed to understand better than most of the most learned heathens) dealt with him, just as he did with Solomon; because he prayed for wisdom in the first place, he added all things else, which were subordinately to be desired. He made him one of the best philosophers, and best husbandmen; and, to adorn and communicate both those faculties, the best poet: he made him, besides all this, a rich man, and a man who desired to be no richer—

'O fortunatus nimium, et bona qui sua novit!'

To be a husbandman, is but a retreat from the city; to be a philosopher, from the world, or rather a retreat from the world, as it is man's, into the world, as it is God's.

But, since nature denies to most men the capacity or appetite, and fortune allows but

to a very few the opportunities or possibility
of applying themselves wholly to philosophy,
the best mixture of human affairs that we can
make are the employments of a country life.
It is, as Columella calls it, 'Res sine dubita-
tione proxima, et quasi consanguinea sapi-
entiæ,' the nearest neighbour, or rather next
in kindred, to philosophy. Varro says, the
principles of it are the same which Ennius
made to be the principles of all nature, Earth,
Water, Air, and the Sun. It does certainly
comprehend more parts of philosophy, than
any one profession, art, or science, in the
world besides: and therefore Cicero says, the
pleasures of a husbandman 'mihi ad sapientis
vitam proxime videntur accedere,' come very
nigh to those of a philosopher. There is no
other sort of life that affords so many branches
of praise to a panegyrist: the utility of it, to
a man's self; the usefulness, or rather necessity, of it to all the rest of mankind; the
innocence, the pleasure, the antiquity, the
dignity.

The utility (I mean plainly the lucre of it) is
not so great, now in our nation, as arises
from merchandise and the trading of the city,
from whence many of the best estates and
chief honours of the kingdom are derived: we
have no men now fetched from the plough
to be made lords, as they were in Rome to
be made consuls and dictators; the reason of
which I conceive to be from an evil custom,

now grown as strong among us as if it were
a law, which is, that no men put their children
to be bred up apprentices in agriculture, as in
other trades, but such who are so poor, that,
when they come to be men, they have not
wherewithal to set up in it, and so can only
farm some small parcel of ground, the rent
of which devours all but the bare subsistence
of the tenant : whilst they who are proprietors
of the land are either too proud, or, for want
of that kind of education, too ignorant, to improve their estates, though the means of doing
it be as easy and certain in this, as in any
other track of commerce. If there were
always two or three thousand youths, for
seven or eight years, bound to this profession,
that they might learn the whole art of it, and
afterwards be enabled to be masters of it, by
a moderate stock; I cannot doubt but that
we should see as many aldermen's estates
made in the country, as now we do out of all
kind of merchandising in the city. There are
as many ways to be rich, and, which is better,
there is no possibility to be poor, without
such negligence as can neither have excuse
nor pity ; for a little ground will, without
question, feed a little family, and the superfluities of life (which are now in some cases
by custom made almost necessary) must be
supplied out of the superabundance of art and
industry, or contemned by as great a degree
of philosophy.

As for the necessity of this art, it is evident enough, since this can live without all others, and no one other without this. This is like speech, without which the society of men cannot be preserved; the others, like figures and tropes of speech, which serve only to adorn it. Many nations have lived, and some do still, without any art but this: not so elegantly, I confess, but still they live; and almost all the other arts, which are here practised, are beholding to this for most of their materials.

The innocence of this life is the next thing for which I commend it; and if husbandmen preserve not that, they are much to blame, for no men are so free from the temptations of iniquity. They live by what they can get by industry from the earth; and others, by what they can catch by craft from men. They live upon an estate given them by their mother; and others, upon an estate cheated from their brethren. They live, like sheep and kine, by the allowances of nature; and others, like wolves and foxes, by the acquisitions of rapine. And, I hope, I may affirm, (without any offence to the great) that sheep and kine are very useful, and that wolves and foxes are pernicious creatures. They are, without dispute, of all men, the most quiet and least apt to be inflamed to the disturbance of the commonwealth: their manner of life inclines them, and interest binds them, to love peace: in our late mad and miserable civil wars, all other trades, even to the meanest, set forth whole troops, and raised up some great commanders, who became famous and mighty for the mischiefs they had done: but I do not remember the name of any one husbandman, who had so considerable a share in the twenty years' ruin of his country, as to deserve the curses of his countrymen.

And if great delights be joined with so much innocence, I think it is ill done of men, not to take them here, where they are so tame, and ready at hand, rather than hunt for them in courts and cities, where they are so wild, and the chase so troublesome and dangerous.

We are here among the vast and noble scenes of nature; we are there among the pitiful shifts of policy: we walk here in the light and open ways of the divine bounty; we grope there in the dark and confused labyrinths of human malice: our senses are here feasted with the clear and genuine taste of their objects, which are all sophisticated there, and for the most part overwhelmed with their contraries. Here, pleasure looks (methinks) like a beautiful, constant, and modest wife; it is there an impudent, fickle, and painted harlot. Here, is harmless and cheap plenty; there, guilty and expenseful luxury.

I shall only instance in one delight more, the most natural and best-natured of all others,

a perpetual companion of the husbandman;
and that is, the satisfaction of looking round
about him, and seeing nothing but the effects
and improvements of his own art and diligence; to be always gathering of some fruits
of it, and at the same time to behold others
ripening, and others budding: to see all his
fields and gardens covered with the beauteous
creatures of his own industry; and to see,
like God, that all his works are good:—

' Hinc atque hinc glomerantur Oreades; ipsi
Agricolæ tacitum pertentant gaudia pectus.'

On his heart-strings a secret joy does strike.

The antiquity of his art is certainly not to
be contested by any other. The three first
men in the world, were a gardener, a plough-
man, and a grazier; and if any man object,
that the second of these was a murderer, I
desire he would consider, that as soon as he
was so, he quitted our profession, and turned
builder. It is for this reason, I suppose, that
Ecclesiasticus forbids us to hate husbandry;
' because (says he) the Most High has created
it.' We were all born to this art, and taught
by nature to nourish our bodies by the same
earth out of which they were made, and to
which they must return, and pay at last for
their sustenance.

Behold the original and primitive nobility
of all those great persons, who are too proud

now, not only to till the ground, but almost
to tread upon it. We may talk what we
please of lilies, and lions rampant, and spread-
eagles, in fields 'd'or' or 'd'argent'; but, if
heraldry were guided by reason, a plough in
a field arable, would be the most noble and
ancient arms.

All these considerations make me fall into
the wonder and complaint of Columella, how
it should come to pass that all arts or sciences
(for the dispute, which is an art, and which is
a science, does not belong to the curiosity of
us husbandmen), metaphysic, physic, morality,
mathematics, logic, rhetoric, etc., which are
all, I grant, good and useful faculties (except
only metaphysic, which I do not know
whether it be anything or no); but even
vaulting, fencing, dancing, attiring, cookery,
carving, and such like vanities, should all
have public schools and masters, and yet that
we should never see or hear of any man, who
took upon him the profession of teaching this
so pleasant, so virtuous, so profitable, so
honourable, so necessary art.

A man would think, when he's in serious
humour, that it were but a vain, irrational,
and ridiculous thing, for a great company of
men and women to run up and down in a
room together, in a hundred several postures
and figures, to no purpose, and with no
design; and therefore dancing was invented
first, and only practised anciently, in the

ceremonies of the heathen religion, which consisted all in mummery and madness; the latter being the chief glory of the worship, and accounted divine inspiration: this, I say, a severe man would think; though I dare not determine so far against so customary a part now, of good-breeding. And yet, who is there among our gentry, that does not entertain a dancing-master for his children, as soon as they are able to walk? But did ever any father provide a tutor for his son, instruct him betimes in the nature and improvements of that land which he intended to leave him? That is at least a superfluity, and this a defect, in our manner of education; and therefore I could wish (but cannot in these times much hope to see it) that one college in each university were erected, and appropriated to this study, as well as there are to medicine and the civil law: there would be no need of making a body of scholars and fellows, with certain endowments, as in other colleges; it would suffice, if, after the manner of halls in Oxford, there were only four professors constituted (for it would be too much work for only one master, or principal, as they call him there) to teach these four parts of it: First, Aration, and all things relating to it. Secondly, Pasturage. Thirdly, Gardens, Orchards, Vineyards, and Woods. Fourthly, all parts of Rural Economy, which would contain the government of Bees, Swine, Poultry, Decoys,

Ponds, etc., and all that which Varro calls 'villaticas pastiones,' together with the sports of the field (which ought to be looked upon not only as pleasures, but as parts of house-keeping), and the domestical conservation and uses of all that is brought in by industry abroad. The business of these professors should not be, as is commonly practised in other arts, only to read pompous and super-ficial lectures, out of Virgil's 'Georgics,' Pliny, Varro, or Columella; but to instruct their pupils in the whole method and course of this study, which might be run through perhaps, with diligence, in a year or two: and the con-tinual succession of scholars, upon a moderate taxation for their diet, lodging, and learning, would be a sufficient, constant revenue for maintenance of the house and the professors, who should be men not chosen for the ostenta-tion of critical literature, but for solid and experimental knowledge of the things they teach; such men, so industrious and public-spirited, as I conceive Mr. Hartlib to be, if the gentleman be yet alive: but it is needless to speak further of my thoughts of this de-sign, unless the present disposition of the age allowed more probability of bringing it into execution. What I have further to say of the country life, shall be borrowed from the poets, who were always the most faithful and affec-tionate friends to it. Poetry was born among the shepherds.

ABRAHAM COWLEY

' Nescio quâ natale solum dulcedine Musas
   Ducit, et immemores non sinit esse sui.'

The Muses still love their own native place ;
'T has secret charms, which nothing can deface.

The truth is, no other place is proper for
their work ; one might as well undertake to
dance in a crowd, as to make good verses in
the midst of noise and tumult.

As well might corn, as verse, in cities grow ;
In vain the thankless glebe we plough and sow;
Against th' unnatural soil in vain we strive ;
'Tis not a ground, in which these plants will
   thrive.

It will bear nothing but the nettles or thorns
of satire, which grow most naturally in the
worst earth ; and therefore almost all poets,
except those who were not able to eat bread
without the bounty of great men, that is,
without what they could get by flattering of
them, have not only withdrawn themselves
from the vices and vanities of the grand
world,
            ' pariter vitiisque jocisque
      Altius humanis exeruere caput,'

into the innocent happiness of a retired life ;
but have commended and adorned nothing so
much by their ever-living poems.   Hesiod
was the first or second poet in the world that
remains yet extant (if Homer, as some think,
preceded him, but I rather believe they were

31

contemporaries); and he is the first writer too
of the art of husbandry: he has contributed
(says Columella) not a little to our profession;
I suppose, he means not a little honour, for
the matter of his instructions is not very important: his great antiquity is visible through
the gravity and simplicity of his style. The
most acute of all his sayings concerns our
purpose very much, and is couched in the
reverend obscurity of an oracle. Πλέον
ἥμισυ παντός, The half is more than the
whole. The occasion of the speech is this:
his brother Perses had, by corrupting some
great men (βασιλῆας δωροφάγους, great
bribe-eaters he calls them), gotten from him
the half of his estate. It is no matter (says
he); they have not done me so much prejudice, as they imagine:

Νήπιοι, οὐδ' ἴσασιν ὅσῳ πλέον ἥμισυ παντός,
Οὐδ' ὅσον ἐν μαλάχῃ τε καὶ ἀσφοδέλῳ μέγ'
ὄνειαρ,
Κρύψαντες γὰρ ἔχουσι θεοὶ βίον ἀνθρώ-
ποισι.

Unhappy they, to whom God has not reveal'd,
By a strong light which must their sense con-
trol,
That half a great estate's more than the whole:
Unhappy, from whom still conceal'd does lie,
Of roots and herbs, the wholesome luxury.

This I conceive to be honest Hesiod's
meaning. From Homer, we must not ex-

pect much concerning our affairs. He was
blind, and could neither work in the country,
nor enjoy the pleasures of it; his helpless
poverty was likeliest to be sustained in the
richest places; he was to delight the Grecians
with fine tales of the wars and adventures of
their ancestors; his subject removed him from
all commerce with us, and yet, methinks, he
made a shift to show his good-will a little.
For, though he could do us no honour in the
person of his hero Ulysses (much less of
Achilles), because his whole time was con-
sumed in wars and voyages; yet he makes
his father Laertes a gardener all that while,
and seeking his consolation for the absence
of his son in the pleasure of planting,
and even dunging his own grounds. Ye
see, he did not contemn us peasants; nay,
so far was he from that insolence, that he
always styles Eumæus, who kept the hogs,
with wonderful respect, δῖον ὕφορβον, the
divine swine herd: he could have done no
more for Menelaus or Agamemnon. And
Theocritus (a very ancient poet, but he was
one of our own tribe, for he wrote nothing
but pastorals) gave the same epithet to an
husbandman,

—ἀμείβετο δῖος ἀγρώτης.

The divine husbandman replied to Hercules,
who was but δῖος himself. These were civil
Greeks, and who understood the dignity of

our calling! Among the Romans we have, in the first place, our truly divine Virgil, who, though, by the favour of Mæcenas and Augustus, he might have been one of the chief men of Rome, yet chose rather to employ much of his time in the exercise, and much of his immortal wit in the praise and instructions, of a rustic life; who, though he had written, before, whole books of pastorals and Georgics, could not abstain, in his great and imperial poem, from describing Evander, one of his best princes, as living just after the homely manner of an ordinary countryman. He seats him in a throne of maple, and lays him but upon a bear's skin; the kine and oxen are lowing in his court-yard; the birds under the eves of his window call him up in the morning; and when he goes abroad, only two dogs go along with him for his guard: at last, when he brings Æneas into his royal cottage, he makes him say this memorable compliment, greater than ever yet was spoken at the Escurial, the Louvre, or our Whitehall:

'Hæc (inquit) limina victor
Alcides subiit, hæc illum regia cepit:
Aude, hospes, contemnere opes: et te quoque
    dignum
Finge Deo, rebusque veni non asper egenis.'

This humble roof, this rustic court, (said he)
Receiv'd Alcides, crown'd with victory:

Scorn not, great guest, the steps where he has
  trod;
But contemn wealth, and imitate a God.

The next man, whom we are much obliged
to, both for his doctrine and example, is the
next best poet in the world to Virgil, his dear
friend Horace; who, when Augustus had
desired Mæcenas to persuade him to come
and live domestically and at the same table
with him, and to be secretary of state of the
whole world under him, or rather jointly with
him, for he says, 'ut nos in epistolis scribendis
adjuvet,' could not be tempted to forsake his
Sabine, or Tiburtin manor, for so rich and
so glorious a trouble. There was never, I
think, such an example as this in the world,
that he should have so much moderation and
courage as to refuse an offer of such greatness, and the emperor so much generosity and
good-nature as not to be at all offended with
his refusal, but to retain still the same kindness, and express it often to him in most
friendly and familiar letters, part of which are
still extant. If I should produce all the
passages of this excellent author upon the
several subjects which I treat of in this book,
I must be obliged to translate half his works;
of which I may say more truly than, in my
opinion, he did of Homer,

'Qui, quid sit pulchrum, quid turpe, quid utile,
  quid non,
Planius et melius Chrysippo et Crantore dicit.'

35

I shall content myself upon this particular
theme, with three only, one out of his Odes,
the other out of his Satires, the third out of
his Epistles; and shall forbear to collect the
suffrages of all other poets, which may be
found scattered up and down through all their
writings, and especially in Martial's. But I
must not omit to make some excuse for the
bold undertaking of my own unskilful pencil
upon the beauties of a face that has been
drawn before by so many great masters;
especially, that I should dare to do it in Latin
verses (though of another kind), and have the
confidence to translate them. I can only say
that I love the matter, and that ought to
cover many faults; and that I run not to
contend with those before me, but follow
to applaud them.

N.B.—We have omitted the poems as not
proper to this anthology.

OF GREATNESS

Since we cannot attain to greatness (says
the Sieur de Montagne), let's have our revenge by railing at it: this he spoke but in
jest. I believe he desired it no more than I
do, and had less reason; for he enjoyed so
plentiful and honourable a fortune in a most
excellent country, as allowed him all the real
conveniences of it, separated and purged

from the incommodities. If I were but in his condition, I should think it hard measure, without being convinced of any crime, to be sequestered from it, and made one of the principal officers of state. But the reader may think that what I now say is of small authority, because I never was, nor ever shall be, put to the trial: I can therefore only make my protestation,

> If ever I more riches did desire,
> Than cleanliness and quiet do require :
> If e'er ambition did my fancy cheat,
> With any wish, so mean as to be great,
> Continue, heaven, still from me to remove
> The humble blessings of that life I love.

I know very many men will despise, and some pity me, for this humour, as a poor-spirited fellow; but I'm content, and, like Horace, thank God for being so.

> 'Di bene fecerunt, inopis me quodque pusilli
> Finxerunt animi.'

I confess, I love littleness almost in all things. A little convenient estate, a little cheerful house, a little company, and a very little feast ; and, if I were to fall in love again (which is a great passion, and therefore, I hope, I have done with it) it would be, I think, with prettiness, rather than with majestical beauty. I would neither wish that my mistress, nor my fortune, should be a 'bona roba,' nor, as Homer uses to describe his beauties, like a daughter of great Jupiter, for the stateliness and largeness of her person; but, as Lucretius says,

'Parvula, pumilio, Χαρίτων μία, tota merum sal.'

Where there is one man of this, I believe there are a thousand of Senecio's mind, whose ridiculous affectation of grandeur, Seneca the elder describes to this effect: Senecio was a man of a turbid and confused wit, who could not endure to speak any but mighty words and sentences, till this humour grew at last into so notorious a habit, or rather disease, as became the sport of the whole town: he would have no servants, but huge, massy fellows; no plate or household stuff, but thrice as big as the fashion: you may believe me, for I speak it without raillery, his extravagancy came at last into such a madness, that he would not put on a pair of shoes, each of which was not big enough for both his feet: he would eat nothing but what was great, nor touch any fruit but horse-plums and pound-pears: his mistress was a very giantess, and he made her walk too always in chiopins, till at last, he got the surname of Senecio Grandio, which, Messala said, was not his 'cognomen,' but his 'cognomentum': when he declaimed for the three hundred Lacedæmonians, who alone opposed Xerxes his army of above three

38

hundred thousand, he stretched out his arms, and stood on tiptoes, that he might appear the taller, and cried out, in a very loud voice: 'I rejoice, I rejoice'—We wondered, I remember, what new great fortune had befallen his eminence. Xerxes (says he) is all mine own. He, who took away the sight of the sea, with the canvas veils of so many ships—and then he goes on so, as I know not what to make of the rest, whether it be the fault of the edition, or the orator's own burly way of nonsense.

This is the character that Seneca gives of this hyperbolical fop, whom we stand amazed at, and yet there are very few men who are not in some things, and to some degrees, 'Grandios.' Is any thing more common, than to see our ladies of quality wear such high shoes as they cannot walk in, without one to lead them: and a gown as long again as their body, so that they cannot stir to the next room, without a page or two to hold it up? I may safely say, that all the ostentation of our grandees is, just like a train, of no use in the world, but horribly cumbersome and incommodious. What is all this, but a spice of 'Grandio'? how tedious would this be, if we were always bound to it! I do believe there is no king, who would not rather be deposed, than endure, every day of his reign, all the ceremonies of his coronation.

The mightiest princes are glad to fly often

from these majestic pleasures (which is, methinks, no small disparagement to them) as it
were for refuge, to the most contemptible
divertisements, and meanest recreations of
the vulgar, nay, even of children. One of the
most powerful and fortunate princes of the
world, of late, could find out no delight so
satisfactory, as the keeping of little singing
birds, and hearing of them, and whistling to
them. What did the emperors of the whole
world? If ever any men had the free and
full enjoyment of all human greatness (nay
that would not suffice, for they would be gods
too), they certainly possessed it: and yet one
of them, who styled himself lord and god of
the earth, could not tell how to pass his whole
day pleasantly, without spending constantly
two or three hours in catching of flies, and kill-
ing them with a bodkin, as if his godship had
been Beelzebub. One of his predecessors,
Nero (who never put any bounds, nor met
with any stop to his appetite), could divert
himself with no pastime more agreeable, than
to run about the streets all night in a disguise,
and abuse the women, and affront the men
whom he met, and sometimes to beat them,
and sometimes to be beaten by them: this
was one of his imperial nocturnal pleasures.
His chiefest in the day was, to sing, and play
upon a fiddle, in the habit of a minstrel, upon
the public stage: he was prouder of the
garlands that were given to his divine voice

ABRAHAM COWLEY

(as they called it then) in those kind of prizes,
than all his forefathers were, of their triumphs
over nations: he did not at his death complain
that so mighty an emperor, and the last of all
the Cæsarian race of deities, should be brought
to so shameful and miserable an end; but
only cried out, 'Alas, what pity 'tis, that so
excellent a musician should perish in this
manner!' His uncle Claudius spent half his
time at playing at dice; that was the main
fruit of his sovereignty. I omit the madnesses
of Caligula's delights, and the execrable
sordidness of those of Tiberius. Would one
think that Augustus himself, the highest and
most fortunate of mankind, a person endowed
too with many excellent parts of nature,
should be so hard put to it sometimes for
want of recreations, as to be found playing at
nuts and bounding-stones, with little Syrian
and Moorish boys, whose company he took
delight in, for their prating and their wantonness?

Was it for this, that Rome's best blood he spilt,
  With so much falsehood, so much guilt?
Was it for this, that his ambition strove
To equal Cæsar first, and after Jove?
Greatness is barren, sure, of solid joys;
Her merchandise (I fear) is all in toys:
She could not else, sure, so uncivil be,
To treat his universal majesty,
His new-created Deity,
With nuts and bounding-stones and boys.

41

But we must excuse her for this meagre entertainment; she has not really wherewithal to make such feasts as we imagine. Her guests must be contented sometimes with but slender cates, and with the same cold meats served over and over again, even till they become nauseous. When you have pared away all the vanity, what solid and natural contentment does there remain, which may not be had with five hundred pounds a year? Not so many servants or horses; but a few good ones, which will do all the business as well: not so many choice dishes at every meal; but at several meals all of them, which makes them both the more healthy, and the more pleasant: not so rich garments, nor so frequent changes; but as warm and as comely, and so frequent change too, as is every jot as good for the master, though not for the tailor or valet de chambre: not such a stately palace, nor gilt rooms, or the costliest sorts of tapestry; but a convenient brick house, with decent wainscot, and pretty, forest-work hangings. Lastly, (for I omit all other particulars, and will end with that which I love most in both conditions) not whole woods cut in walks, nor vast parks, nor fountain or cascade gardens; but herb, and flower, and fruit gardens, which are more useful, and the water every whit as clear and wholesome as if it darted from the breasts of a marble nymph, or the urn of a river-god.

If, for all this, you like better the substance
of that former estate of life, do but consider
the inseparable accidents of both: servitude,
disquiet, danger, and, most commonly, guilt,
inherent in the one; in the other, liberty,
tranquillity, security, and innocence. And
when you have thought upon this, you will
confess that to be a truth which appeared to
you, before, but a ridiculous paradox, that a
low fortune is better guarded and attended
than a high one. If, indeed, we look only
upon the flourishing head of the tree, it
appears a most beautiful object,

> 'sed quantum vertice ad auras
> Ætherias, tantum radice in Tartara tendit.'

As far as up tow'rds heaven the branches
    grow,
So far the roots sink down to hell below.

Another horrible disgrace to greatness is,
that it is for the most part in pitiful want and
distress. What a wonderful thing is this!
Unless it degenerate into avarice, and so
cease to be greatness, it falls perpetually into
such necessities, as drive it into all the meanest and most sordid ways of borrowing,
cozenage, and robbery:

'Mancipiis locuples, eget æris Cappadocum
    rex.'

This is the case of almost all great men, as
well as of the poor king of Cappadocia: they

43

abound with slaves, but are indigent of
money. The ancient Roman emperors, who
had the riches of the whole world for their
revenue, had wherewithal to live (one would
have thought) pretty well at ease, and to have
been exempt from the pressures of extreme
poverty. But, yet with most of them it was
much otherwise; and they fell perpetually
into such miserable penury, that they were
forced to devour or squeeze most of their
friends and servants, to cheat with infamous
projects, to ransack and pillage all their
provinces. This fashion of imperial grandeur
is imitated by all inferior and subordinate sorts
of it, as if it were a point of honour. They
must be cheated of a third part of their
estates; two other thirds they must expend
in vanity; so that they remain debtors for all
the necessary provisions of life, and have no
way to satisfy those debts, but out of the
succours and supplies of rapine: 'as riches
increase' (says Solomon), 'so do the mouths
that devour them.' The master mouth has
no more than before. The owner, methinks,
is like Ocnus in the fable, who is perpetually
winding a rope of hay, and an ass at the end
perpetually eating it.

Out of these inconveniences arises naturally
one more, which is, that no greatness can be
satisfied or contented with itself: still, if it
could mount up a little higher, it would be
happy; if it could gain but that point, it would

obtain all its desires; but yet at last, when it is got up to the very top of the Peak of Teneriffe, it is in very great danger of breaking its neck downwards, but in no possibility of ascending upwards into the seat of tranquillity above the moon. The first ambitious men in the world, the old giants, are said to have made an heroical attempt of scaling heaven in despite of the Gods; and they cast Ossa upon Olympus, and Pelion upon Ossa: two or three mountains more, they thought, would have done their business; but the thunder spoilt all the work when they were come up to the third story:

> And what a noble plot was crost,
> And what a brave design was lost!

A famous person of their offspring, the late giant of our nation, when, from the condition of a very inconsiderable captain, he made himself lieutenant-general of an army of little Titans, which was his first mountain, and afterwards general, which was his second, and after that, absolute tyrant of three kingdoms, which was the third, and almost touched the heaven which he affected, is believed to have died with grief and discontent, because he could not attain to the honest name of a king, and the old formality of a crown, though he had before exceeded the power by a wicked usurpation. If he could have compassed that, he would per-

45

haps have wanted something else that is
necessary to felicity, and pined away for the
want of the title of an emperor or a god.
The reason of this is, that greatness has no
reality in nature, but is a creature of the
fancy, a notion that consists only in relation
and comparison: it is indeed an idol: but
St. Paul teaches us, 'that an idol is nothing
in the world.' There is, in truth, no rising or
meridian of the sun, but only in respect to
several places: there is no right or left, no
upper-hand, in nature; every thing is little,
and every thing is great, according as it is
diversely compared. There may be perhaps
some village in Scotland or Ireland, where I
might be a great man; and in that case I
should be like Cæsar (you would wonder how
Cæsar and I should be like one another in
any thing), and choose rather to be the first
man of the village, than second at Rome.
Our country is called Great Brittany, in regard
only of a lesser of the same name; it would
be but a ridiculous epithet for it, when we
consider it together with the kingdom of
China. That, too, is but a pitiful rood of
ground, in comparison of the whole earth
besides: and this whole globe of earth, which
we account so immense a body, is but one
point or atom in relation to those numberless worlds that are scattered up and down
in the infinite space of the sky which we
behold.

ABRAHAM COWLEY

THE DANGERS OF AN HONEST MAN
IN MUCH COMPANY

If twenty thousand naked Americans were
not able to resist the assaults of but twenty
well-armed Spaniards, I see little possibility
for one honest man to defend himself against
twenty thousand knaves, who are all furnished
cap-a-pe, with the defensive arms of worldly
prudence, and the offensive, too, of craft and
malice.   He will find no less odds than this
against him, if he have much to do in human
affairs.   The only advice therefore which I
can give him is, to be sure not to venture his
person any longer in the open campaign, to
retreat and entrench himself, to stop up all
avenues, and draw up all bridges against so
numerous an enemy.

The truth of it is, that a man in much business must either make himself a knave, or
else the world will make him a fool: and, if
the injury went no farther than the being
laughed at, a wise man would content himself
with the revenge of retaliation ; but the case
is much worse, for these civil cannibals, too,
as well as the wild ones, not only dance
about such a taking stranger, but at last
devour him.   A sober man cannot get too
soon out of drunken company, though they
be never so kind and merry among them-

47

selves; 'tis not unpleasant only, but dangerous to him.

Do ye wonder that a virtuous man should love to be alone? It is hard for him to be otherwise; he is so, when he is among ten thousand: neither is the solitude so uncomfortable to be alone without any other creature, as it is to be alone in the midst of wild beasts. Man is to man all kind of beasts; a fawning dog, a roaring lion, a thieving fox, a robbing wolf, a dissembling crocodile, a treacherous decoy, and a rapacious vulture. The civilest, methinks, of all nations, are those, whom we account the most barbarous; there is some moderation and good-nature in the Toupinambaltians, who eat no men but their enemies, whilst we learned and polite and Christian Europeans, like so many pikes and sharks, prey upon everything that we can swallow. It is the great boast of eloquence and philosophy, that they first congregated men dispersed, united them into societies, and built up the houses and the walls of cities. I wish, they could unravel all they had woven; that we might have our woods and our innocence again, instead of our castles and our policies. They have assembled many thousands of scattered people into one body: 'tis true, they have done so; they have brought them into cities to cozen, and into armies to murder one another: they found them hunters and fishers of wild creatures; they have made them hunters and fishers of their brethren; they boast to have reduced them to a state of peace, when the truth is, they have only taught them an art of war; they have framed, I must confess, wholesome laws for the restraint of vice, but they raised first that devil, which now they conjure and cannot bind; though there were before no punishments for wickedness, yet there was less committed, because there were no rewards for it.

But the men, who praise philosophy from this topic, are much deceived; let oratory answer for itself, the tinkling perhaps of that may unite a swarm: it never was the work of philosophy to assemble multitudes, but to regulate only, and govern them, when they were assembled; to make the best of an evil, and bring them, as much as is possible, to unity again. Avarice and ambition only were the first builders of towns, and founders of empire; they said, 'Go to, let us build us a city and a tower whose top may reach unto heaven, and let us make a name, lest we be scattered abroad upon the face of the earth.' What was the beginning of Rome, the metropolis of all the world? what was it, but a concourse of thieves, and a sanctuary of criminals? It was justly named by the augury of no less than twelve vultures, and the founder cemented his walls with the blood of his brother. Not unlike to this was the

D   49

beginning even of the first town too in the
world, and such is the original sin of most
cities: their actual increase daily with their
age and growth: the more people, the more
wicked all of them; every one brings in his
part to inflame the contagion, which becomes
at last so universal and so strong, that no
precepts can be sufficient preservatives, nor
anything secure our safety, but flight from
among the infected.

We ought, in the choice of a situation, to
regard, above all things, the healthfulness of
the place, and the healthfulness of it for the
mind, rather than for the body. But suppose
(which is hardly to be supposed) we had anti-
dote enough against this poison; nay, suppose
further, we were always and at all pieces
armed and provided, both against the assaults
of hostility, and the mines of treachery, 'twill
yet be but an uncomfortable life to be ever in
alarms; though we were compassed round
with fire, to defend ourselves from wild beasts,
the lodging would be unpleasant, because we
must always be obliged to watch that fire,
and to fear no less the defects of our guard,
than the diligence of our enemy. The sum of
this is, that a virtuous man is in danger to be
trod upon and destroyed in the crowd of his
contraries, nay, which is worse, to be changed
and corrupted by them; and that 'tis impossible to escape both these inconveniences
without so much caution, as will take away

ABRAHAM COWLEY

the whole quiet, that is, the happiness, of his
life.

Ye see, then, what he may lose; but, I
pray, what can he get there?

'Quid Romæ faciam? Mentiri nescio.'

What should a man of truth and honesty do
at Rome? He can neither understand nor
speak the language of the place; a naked
man may swim in the sea, but 'tis not the way
to catch fish there; they are likelier to devour
him, than he them, if he bring no nets, and
use no deceits. I think, therefore, it was wise
and friendly advice, which Martial gave to
Fabian, when he met him newly arrived at
Rome:

Honest and poor, faithful in word and thought;
What has thee, Fabian, to the city brought?
Thou neither the buffoon nor bawd canst play,
Nor with false whispers th' innocent betray;
Nor with vain promises and projects cheat,
Nor bribe or flatter any of the great.
But you 're a man of learning, prudent, just;
A man of courage, firm, and fit for trust.
Why you may stay, and live unenvied here;
But (faith) go back, and keep you where you
    were.

Nay, if nothing of all this were in the
case, yet the very sight of uncleanness is
loathsome to the cleanly; the sight of folly
and impiety, vexatious to the wise and
pious.

51

Lucretius, by his favour, though a good poet, was but an ill-natured man, when he said, it was delightful to see other men in a great storm, and no less ill-natured should I think Democritus, who laughed at all the world, but that he retired himself so much out of it, that we may perceive he took no great pleasure in that kind of mirth. I have been drawn twice or thrice by company to go to Bedlam, and have seen others very much delighted with the fantastical extravagancy of so many various madnesses, which upon me wrought so contrary an effect, that I always returned, not only melancholy, but even sick with the sight. My compassion there was perhaps too tender, for I meet a thousand madmen abroad, without any perturbation; though to weigh the matter justly, the total loss of reason is less deplorable than the total depravation of it. An exact judge of human blessings, of riches, honours, beauty, even of wit itself, should pity the abuse of them, more than the want.

Briefly, though a wise man could pass never so securely through the great roads of human life, yet he will meet perpetually with so many objects and occasions of compassion, grief, shame, anger, hatred, indignation, and all passions but envy (for he will find nothing to deserve that), that he had better strike into some private path; nay, go so far, if he could, out of the common way, 'ut nec facta audiat

Pelopidarum'; that he might not so much as
hear of the actions of the sons of Adam. But,
whither shall we fly then? into the deserts
like the ancient Hermits?

> 'Qua terra patet, fera regnat Erinnys,
> In facinus jurâsse putes.'

One would think that all mankind had
bound themselves by an oath to do all the
wickedness they can; that they had all (as
the Scripture speaks) 'sold themselves to
sin': the difference only is, that some are
a little more crafty (and but a little, God
knows), in making of the bargain. I thought,
when I went first to dwell in the country,
that, without doubt, I should have met there
with the simplicity of the old poetical golden
age; I thought to have found no inhabitants
there, but such as the shepherds of Sir Philip
Sydney in Arcadia, or of Monsieur d'Urfé
upon the banks of Lignon; and began to
consider with myself, which way I might
recommend no less to posterity the happiness and innocence of the Men of Chertsey:
but, to confess the truth, I perceived quickly,
by infallible demonstrations, that I was still
in Old England, and not in Arcadia, or La
Forrest; that, if I could not content myself
with any thing less than exact fidelity in
human conversation, I had almost as good
go back and seek for it in the Court, or the
Exchange, or Westminster-hall. I ask again

then, whither shall we fly, or what shall we do? The world may so come in a man's way, that he cannot choose but salute it; he must take heed, though, not to go a whoring after it. If, by any lawful vocation, or just necessity, men happen to be married to it, I can only give them St. Paul's advice: 'Brethren, the time is short; it remains, that they, that have wives, be as though they had none.—But I would that all men were even as I myself.'

In all cases, they must be sure, that they do 'mundum ducere,' and not 'mundo nubere.' They must retain the superiority and headship over it; happy are they, who can get out of the sight of this deceitful beauty, that they may not be led so much as into temptation; who have not only quitted the metropolis, but can abstain from ever seeing the next market town of their country.

JOHN DRYDEN

PREFACE TO 'ALL FOR LOVE'

The death of Antony and Cleopatra is a
subject which has been treated by the greatest
wits of our nation, after Shakespeare ; and by
all so variously, that their example has given
me the confidence to try myself in this bow of
Ulysses amongst the crowd of shooters ; and,
withal, to take my own measures, in aiming
at the mark. I doubt not but the same motive
has prevailed with all of us in this attempt ;
I mean the excellency of the moral : for, the
chief persons represented were famous patterns of unlawful love ; and their end accordingly was unfortunate. All reasonable men
have long since concluded, that the hero of
the poem ought not to be a character of perfect virtue, for then he could not, without injustice, be made unhappy ; nor yet altogether
wicked, because he could not then be pitied.
I have therefore steered the middle course ;
and have drawn the character of Antony as
favourably as Plutarch, Appian, and Dion
Cassius would give me leave : the like I have

observed in Cleopatra. That which is wanting to work up the pity to a greater height,
was not afforded me by the story: for the
crimes of love which they both committed,
were not occasioned by any necessity, or fatal
ignorance, but were wholly voluntary; since
our passions are, or ought to be, within our
power. The fabric of the play is regular
enough, as to the inferior parts of it; and
the unities of time, place, and action, more
exactly observed, than, perhaps, the English
theatre requires. Particularly, the action is so
much one, that it is the only one of the kind
without episode, or underplot; every scene in
the tragedy conducing to the main design,
and every act concluding with a turn of it.
The greatest error in the contrivance seems
to be in the person of Octavia: for, though I
might use the privilege of a poet, to introduce
her into Alexandria, yet I had not enough
considered, that the compassion she moved to
herself and children, was destructive to that
which I reserved for Antony and Cleopatra;
whose mutual love being founded upon vice,
must lessen the favour of the audience to
them, when virtue and innocence were oppressed by it. And, though I justified Antony
in some measure, by making Octavia's de-
parture to proceed wholly from herself; yet
the force of the first machine still remained;
and the dividing of pity, like the cutting of a
river into many channels, abated the strength

of the natural stream. But this is an objection which none of my critics have urged against me; and therefore I might have let it pass, if I could have resolved to have been partial to myself. The faults my enemies have found, are rather cavils concerning little, and not essential decencies; which a master of the ceremonies may decide betwixt us. The French poets, I confess, are strict observers of these punctilios: They would not, for example, have suffered Cleopatra and Octavia to have met; or if they had met, there must only have passed betwixt them some cold civilities, but no eagerness of repartee, for fear of offending against the greatness of their characters, and the modesty of their sex. This objection I foresaw, and at the same time contemned: for I judged it both natural and probable, that Octavia, proud of her new-gained conquest, would search out Cleopatra to triumph over her; and that Cleopatra thus attacked, was not of a spirit to shun the encounter: and 'tis not unlikely, that two exasperated rivals should use such satire as I have put into their mouths; for after all, though the one were a Roman, and the other a queen, they were both women. 'Tis true, some actions, though natural, are not fit to be represented; and broad obscenities in words, ought in good manners to be avoided: expressions therefore are a modest clothing of our thoughts, as breeches and petticoats are

57

of our bodies. If I have kept myself within
the bounds of modesty, all beyond it is but
nicety and affectation; which is no more but
modesty depraved into a vice: they betray
themselves who are too quick of apprehen-
sion in such cases, and leave all reasonable
men to imagine worse of them, than of the
poet.

Honest Montaigne goes yet farther:—
'Nous ne sommes que ceremonie; la ceremonie nous emporte, et laissons la substance
des choses: nous nous tenons aux branches,
et abandonnons le tronc et le corps. Nous
avons appris aux dames de rougir, oyans
seulement nommer ce qu'elles ne craignent
aucunement à faire: nous n'osons appeler à
droict nos membres, et ne craignons pas de
les employer à toute sorte de debauche. La
ceremonie nous defend d'exprimer par paroles
les choses licites et naturelles, et nous l'en
croyons, la raison nous defend de n'en faire
point d'illicites et mauvaises, et personne ne
l'en croid.' My comfort is, that by this opinion
my enemies are but sucking critics, who
would fain be nibbling ere their teeth are
come.

Yet, in this nicety of manners does the excellency of French poetry consist: their
heroes are the most civil people breathing;
but their good breeding seldom extends to
a word of sense: all their wit is in their
ceremony; they want the genius which ani-

mates our stage; and therefore 'tis but necessary when they cannot please, that they should
take care not to offend. But, as the civilest
man in the company is commonly the dullest,
so these authors, while they are afraid to
make you laugh or cry, out of pure good
manners, make you sleep. They are so careful not to exasperate a critic, that they never
leave him any work; so busy with the broom,
and make so clean a riddance, that there is
little left either for censure or for praise: for
no part of a poem is worth our discommend-
ing, where the whole is insipid; as when we
have once tasted of palled wine, we stay not
to examine it glass by glass. But while they
affect to shine in trifles, they are often careless
in essentials. Thus their Hippolytus is so
scrupulous in point of decency, that he will
rather expose himself to death, than accuse
his step-mother to his father; and my critics I
am sure will commend him for it: but we of
grosser apprehensions, are apt to think that
this excess of generosity is not practicable
but with fools and madmen. This was good
manners with a vengeance; and the audience
is like to be much concerned at the misfortunes of this admirable hero: but take Hippolytus out of his poetic fit, and I suppose he
would think it a wiser part, to set the saddle
on the right horse, and choose rather to live
with the reputation of a plain-spoken honest
man, than to die with the infamy of an in-

cestuous villain. In the meantime we may take notice, that where the poet ought to have preserved the character as it was delivered to us by antiquity, when he should have given us the picture of a rough young man, of the Amazonian strain, a jolly huntsman, and both by his profession and his early rising a mortal enemy to love, he has chosen to give him the turn of gallantry, sent him to travel from Athens to Paris, taught him to make love, and transformed the Hippolytus of Euripides into Monsieur Hippolite. I should not have troubled myself thus far with French poets, but that I find our Chedreux critics wholly form their judgments by them. But for my part, I desire to be tried by the laws of my own country; for it seems unjust to me, that the French should prescribe here, until they have conquered. Our little sonneteers who follow them, have too narrow souls to judge of poetry. Poets themselves are the most proper, though I conclude not the only critics. But until some genius, as universal as Aristotle, shall arise, one who can penetrate into all arts and sciences, without the practice of them, I shall think it reasonable, that the judgment of an artificer in his own art should be preferable to the opinion of another man; at least where he is not bribed by interest, or prejudiced by malice; and this, I suppose, is manifest by plain induction. For, first, the crowd cannot be presumed to

have more than a gross instinct, of what
pleases or displeases them: every man will
grant me this; but then, by a particular kindness to himself, he draws his own stake first,
and will be distinguished from the multitude,
of which other men may think him one. But,
if I come closer to those who are allowed for
witty men, either by the advantage of their
quality, or by common fame, and affirm that
neither are they qualified to decide sovereignly
concerning poetry, I shall yet have a strong
party of my opinion; for most of them sever-
ally will exclude the rest, either from the
number of witty men, or at least of able
judges. But here again they are all indulgent
to themselves: and every one who believes
himself a wit, that is every man, will pretend
at the same time to a right of judging. But
to press it yet farther, there are many witty
men, but few poets; neither have all poets a
taste of tragedy. And this is the rock on
which they are daily splitting. Poetry, which
is a picture of nature, must generally please:
but it is not to be understood that all parts of
it must please every man; therefore is not
tragedy to be judged by a witty man, whose
taste is only confined to comedy. Nor is
every man who loves tragedy, a sufficient
judge of it: he must understand the excellences of it too, or he will only prove a blind
admirer, not a critic. From hence it comes
that so many satires on poets, and censures of

61

their writings, fly abroad. Men of pleasant
conversation (at least esteemed so), and
endued with a trifling kind of fancy, perhaps helped out with some smattering of
Latin, are ambitious to distinguish themselves from the herd of gentlemen, by their
poetry:

> 'Rarus enim fermè sensus communis in illâ
> Fortunâ.'

And is not this a wretched affectation, not
to be contented with what fortune has done
for them, and sit down quietly with their estates, but they must call their wits in question,
and needlessly expose their nakedness to
public view? Not considering that they are
not to expect the same approbation from
sober men, which they have found from their
flatterers after the third bottle? If a little
glittering in discourse has passed them on us
for witty men, where was the necessity of un-
deceiving the world? Would a man who has
an ill title to an estate, but yet is in possession
of it, would he bring it of his own accord, to
be tried at Westminster? We who write, if
we want the talent, yet have the excuse that
we do it for a poor subsistence: but what can
be urged in their defence, who not having the
vocation of poverty to scribble, out of mere
wantonness take pains to make themselves
ridiculous? Horace was certainly in the
right, where he said, that 'no man is satisfied

with his own condition.' A poet is not pleased because he is not rich; and the rich are discontented, because the poets will not admit them of their number. Thus the case is hard with writers: if they succeed not, they must starve; and if they do, some malicious satire is prepared to level them for daring to please without their leave. But while they are so eager to destroy the fame of others, their ambition is manifest in their concernment: some poem of their own is to be produced, and the slaves are to be laid flat with their faces on the ground, that the monarch may appear in the greater majesty.

Dionysius and Nero had the same longings, but with all their power they could never bring their business well about. It is true, they proclaimed themselves poets by sound of trumpet; and poets they were upon pain of death to any man who durst call them otherwise. The audience had a fine time of it, you may imagine; they sat in a bodily fear, and looked as demurely as they could: for 'twas a hanging matter to laugh unseasonably; and the tyrants were suspicious, as they had reason, that their subjects had 'em in the wind: so, every man in his own defence set as good a face upon the business as he could: it was known beforehand that the monarchs were to be crowned laureates; but when the show was over, and an honest man was suffered to depart quietly, he took out his

laughter which he had stifled ; with a firm
resolution never more to see an emperor's
play, though he had been ten years a making
it. In the meantime, the true poets were they
who made the best markets, for they had wit
enough to yield the prize with a good grace,
and not contend with him who had thirty
legions: they were sure to be rewarded if
they confessed themselves bad writers, and
that was somewhat better than to be martyrs
for their reputation. Lucan's example was
enough to teach them manners ; and after he
was put to death, for overcoming Nero, the
emperor carried it without dispute for the best
poet in his dominions: no man was ambitious
of that grinning honour ; for if he heard the
malicious trumpeter proclaiming his name before his betters, he knew there was but one
way with him. Mecaenas took another
course, and we know he was more than a
great man, for he was witty too: but finding
himself far gone in poetry, which Seneca
assures us was not his talent, he thought it
his best way to be well with Virgil and with
Horace ; that at least he might be a poet at
the second hand ; and we see how happily it
has succeeded with him ; for his own bad
poetry is forgotten, and their panegyrics of
him still remain. But they who would be our
patrons, are for no such expensive ways to
fame. They have much of the poetry of
Mecaenas, but little of his liberality. They

are for persecuting Horace and Virgil, in the
persons of their successors (for such is every
man, who has any part of their soul and fire,
though in a less degree). Some of their little
Zanies yet go farther ; for they are persecutors
even of Horace himself, as far as they are
able, by their ignorant and vile imitations of
him ; by making an unjust use of his authority,
and turning his artillery against his friends.
But how would he disdain to be copied by
such hands ! I dare answer for him, he would
be more uneasy in their company, than he
was with Crispinus, their forefather in the
holy way ; and would no more have allowed
them a place amongst the critics, than he
would Demetrius the mimic, and Tigellius the
buffoon :

<blockquote>
' Demetri, teque Tigelli,
Discipulorum inter jubeo plorare Cathedras.'
</blockquote>

With what scorn would he look down on
such miserable translators, who make dog-
gerel of his Latin, mistake his meaning, mis-
apply his censures, and often contradict their
own ? He is fixed as a landmark to set out
the bounds of poetry :

<blockquote>
' Saxum antiquum, ingens
Limes agra positus, litem ut descerneret
arvis : '
</blockquote>

But other arms than theirs, and other sinews
are required, to raise the weight of such an

E   65

author; and when they would toss him
against their enemies :

> 'Genua labant, gelidus concevit frigore san-
> guis,
> Tum lapis ipse viri, vacuum per inane vo-
> lutus,
> Nec spatium evasit totum, nec pertulit
> ictum.'

For my part, I would wish no other revenge, either for myself or the rest of the
poets, from this rhyming judge of the twelve-
penny gallery, this legitimate son of Sternhold,
than that he would subscribe his name to his
censure, or (not to tax him beyond his learning) set his mark : for should he own himself
publicly, and come from behind the lion's skin,
they whom he condemns would be thankful to
him, they whom he praises would choose to
be condemned ; and the magistrates whom he
has elected, would modestly withdraw from
their employment, to avoid the scandal of his
nomination. The sharpness of his satire,
next to himself, falls most heavily on his
friends, and they ought never to forgive him
for commending them perpetually the wrong
way, and sometimes by contraries. If he
have a friend whose hastiness in writing is
his greatest fault, Horace would have taught
him to have minced the matter, and to have
called it readiness of thought, and a flowing
fancy : for friendship will allow a man to

christen an imperfection by the name of some
neighbour virtue:

'Vellem in amicitiâ sic erraremus et isti
Errori nomen virtus posuisset honestum.'

But he would never have allowed him to have
called a slow man hasty, or a hasty writer a
slow drudge, as Juvenal explains it:

'Canibus pigris, scabieque vetustâ
Levibus, et siccae labentibus ora lucernae,
Nomen erit, Pardus, Tygris, Leo; si quid
adhuc est
Quod fremat in terris violentius.'

Yet Lucretius laughs at a foolish lover,
even for excusing the imperfections of his
mistress:

'Nigra μιλίχροος est, immunda et foetida
ἄκοσμος,
Balba loqui non quit, τραυλίζει; muta pu-
dens est, etc.'

But to drive it 'ad Aethiopem Cygnum' is
not to be endured. I leave him to interpret
this by the benefit of his French version on
the other side, and without farther considering him, than I have the rest of my illiterate
censors, whom I have disdained to answer,
because they are not qualified for judges. It
remains that I acquaint the reader, that I have
endeavoured in this play to follow the practice
of the ancients, who, as Mr. Rymer has

judiciously observed, are and ought to be our masters. Horace likewise gives it for a rule in his 'Art of Poetry':

'Vos exemplaria Graeca
Nocturnâ versate manu, versate diurnâ.'

Yet, though their models are regular, they are too little for English tragedy; which requires to be built in a larger compass. I could give an instance in the 'Oedipus Tyrannus,' which was the masterpiece of Sophocles; but I reserve it for a more fit occasion, which I hope to have hereafter. In my style I have professed to imitate the divine Shakespeare; which that I might perform more freely, I have disencumbered myself from rhyme. Not that I condemn my former way, but that this is more proper to my present purpose. I hope I need not to explain myself, that I have not copied my author servilely: words and phrases must of necessity receive a change in succeeding ages: but 'tis almost a miracle that much of his language remains so pure; and that he who began dramatic poetry amongst us, untaught by any, and, as Ben Jonson tells us, without learning, should by the force of his own genius, perform so much, that in a manner he has left no praise for any who come after him. The occasion is fair, and the subject would be pleasant, to handle the difference of styles betwixt him and Fletcher, and wherein, and how far they are both to be imitated. But since I must not be over-confident of my own performance after him, it will be prudence in me to be silent. Yet, I hope, I may affirm, and without vanity, that by imitating him, I have excelled myself throughout the play; and particularly, that I prefer the scene betwixt Antony and Ventidius in the first act, to anything which I have written in this kind.

THE PREFACE TO 'RELIGIO LAICI'

A poem with so bold a title, and a name prefixed from which the handling of so serious a subject would not be expected, may reasonably oblige the author to say somewhat in defence both of himself and of his undertaking. In the first place, if it be objected to me that, being a layman, I ought not to have concerned myself with speculations which belong to the profession of divinity, I could answer that perhaps laymen, with equal advantages, of parts and knowledge, are not the most incompetent judges of sacred things: but in the due sense of my own weakness and want of learning I plead not this; I pretend not to make myself a judge of faith in others, but only to make a confession of my own. I lay no unhallowed hand upon the Ark, but wait on it with the reverence that becomes me at a distance.

In the next place, I will ingenuously confess
that the helps I have used in this small
Treatise were many of them taken from the
works of our own reverend divines of the
Church of England; so that the weapons
with which I combat irreligion are already
consecrated, though I suppose they may be
taken down as lawfully as the sword of
Goliah was by David, when they are to be
employed for the common cause against the
enemies of piety. I intend not by this to
entitle them to any of my errors, which yet
I hope are only those of charity to mankind;
and such as my own charity has caused me
to commit, that of others may more easily
excuse. Being naturally inclined to scepticism
in philosophy, I have no reason to impose my
opinions in a subject which is above it; but,
whatever they are, I submit them with all
reverence to my mother Church, accounting
them no farther mine, than as they are
authorised or at least uncondemned by her.
And, indeed, to secure myself on this side,
I have used the necessary precaution of
showing this paper, because it was published,
to a judicious and learned friend, a man inde-
fatigably zealous in the service of the Church
and State, and whose writings have highly
deserved of both. He was pleased to approve
the body of the discourse, and I hope he is
more my friend than to do it out of com-
plaisance; 'tis true he had too good a taste

to like it all; and amongst some other faults
recommended to my second view what I have
written perhaps too boldly on St. Athanasius,
which he advised me wholly to omit. I am
sensible enough that I had done more prudently to have followed his opinion; but then
I could not have satisfied myself that I had
done honestly not to have written what was
my own. It has always been my thought,
that heathens who never did, nor without
miracle could, hear of the name of Christ,
were yet in a possibility of salvation. Neither
will it enter easily into my belief, that before
the coming of our Saviour the whole world,
excepting only the Jewish nation, should lie
under the inevitable necessity of everlasting
punishment, for want of that Revelation,
which was confined to so small a spot of
ground as that of Palestine. Among the
sons of Noah we read of one only who was
accursed; and if a blessing in the ripeness
of time was reserved for Japhet (of whose
progeny we are), it seems unaccountable to
me, why so many generations of the same
offspring as preceded our Saviour in the flesh
should be all involved in one common con-
demnation, and yet that their posterity should
be entitled to the hopes of salvation: as if
a Bill of Exclusion had passed only on the
fathers, which debarred not the sons from
their succession; or that so many ages had
been delivered over to Hell, and so many

reserved for Heaven, and that the Devil had
the first choice, and God the next. Truly
I am apt to think that the revealed religion
which was taught by Noah to all his sons
might continue for some ages in the whole
posterity. That afterwards it was included
wholly in the family of Shem is manifest;
but when the progenies of Cham and Japhet
swarmed into colonies, and those colonies
were subdivided into many others, in process
of time their descendants lost by little and
little the primitive and purer rites of divine
worship, retaining only the notion of one
deity; to which succeeding generations added
others; for men took their degrees in those
ages from conquerors to gods. Revelation
being thus eclipsed to almost all mankind,
the Light of Nature, as the next in dignity,
was substituted; and that is it which
St. Paul concludes to be the rule of the
heathens, and by which they are hereafter
to be judged. If my supposition be true,
then the consequence which I have assumed
in my poem may be also true; namely, that
Deism, or the principles of natural worship,
are only the faint remnants or dying flames
of revealed religion in the posterity of Noah:
and that our modern philosophers, nay, and
some of our philosophising divines, have too
much exalted the faculties of our souls, when
they have maintained that by their force mankind has been able to find out that there is

one supreme agent or intellectual Being
which we call God; that praise and prayer
are his due worship; and the rest of those
deducements, which I am confident are the
remote effects of Revelation, and unattain-
able by our Discourse, I mean as simply
considered, and without the benefit of divine
illumination. So that we have not lifted up
ourselves to God by the weak pinions of our
Reason, but he has been pleased to descend
to us; and what Socrates said of him, what
Plato writ, and the rest of the heathen
philosophers of several nations, is all no more
than the twilight of Revelation, after the sun
of it was set in the race of Noah. That
there is something above us, some principle
of motion, our Reason can apprehend, though
it cannot discover what it is by its own
virtue. And, indeed, 'tis very improbable
that we, who by the strength of our faculties
cannot enter into the knowledge of any
being, not so much as of our own, should
be able to find out by them that supreme
nature, which we cannot otherwise define
than by saying it is infinite; as if infinite
were definable, or infinity a subject for our
narrow understanding. They who would
prove religion by reason do but weaken the
cause which they endeavour to support: 'tis
to take away the pillars from our faith, and
to prop it only with a twig; 'tis to design
a tower like that of Babel, which, if it were

possible (as it is not) to reach heaven, would come to nothing by the confusion of the workmen. For every man is building a several way; impotently conceited of his own model and his own materials: reason is always striving, and always at a loss; and of necessity it must so come to pass, while 'tis exercised about that which is not its proper object. Let us be content at last to know God by his own methods; at least, so much of him as he is pleased to reveal to us in the sacred Scriptures: to apprehend them to be the word of God is all our reason has to do; for all beyond it is the work of faith, which is the seal of Heaven impressed upon our human understanding.

And now for what concerns the holy bishop Athanasius, the Preface of whose Creed seems inconsistent with my opinion, which is, that heathens may possibly be saved: in the first place, I desire it may be considered that it is the Preface only, not the Creed itself, which, till I am better informed, is of too hard a digestion for my charity. It is not that I am ignorant how many several texts of Scripture seemingly support that cause; but neither am I ignorant how all those texts may receive a kinder and more mollified interpretation. Every man who is read in Church history knows that Belief was drawn up after a long contestation with Arius concerning the divinity of our blessed

Saviour and his being one substance with the Father; and that, thus compiled, it was sent abroad among the Christian churches, as a kind of test, which whosoever took was looked on as an orthodox believer. It is manifest from hence, that the heathen part of the empire was not concerned in it; for its business was not to distinguish betwixt Pagans and Christians, but betwixt heretics and true believers. This, well considered, takes off the heavy weight of censure, which I would willingly avoid from so venerable a man; for if this proportion, 'whosoever will be saved,' be restrained only to those to whom it was intended, and for whom it was composed, I mean the Christians, then the anathema reaches not the heathens, who had never heard of Christ and were nothing interested in that dispute. After all, I am far from blaming even that prefatory addition to the creed, and as far from cavilling at the continuation of it in the Liturgy of the Church, where on the days appointed 'tis publicly read: for I suppose there is the same reason for it now in opposition to the Socinians as there was then against the Arians; the one being a heresy, which seems to have been refined out of the other; and with how much more plausibility of reason it combats our religion, with so much more caution to be avoided: and therefore the prudence of our church is to be commended, which has interposed her authority for the recommendation of this Creed. Yet to such as are grounded in the true belief, those explanatory Creeds, the Nicene and this of Athanasius, might perhaps be spared; for what is supernatural will always be a mystery in spite of exposition, and for my own part, the plain Apostles' Creed is most suitable to my weak understanding, as the simplest diet is the most easy of digestion.

I have dwelt longer on this subject than I intended, and longer than perhaps I ought; for having laid down, as my foundation, that the Scripture is a rule, that in all things needful to salvation it is clear, sufficient, and ordained by God Almighty for that purpose, I have left myself no right to interpret obscure places, such as concern the possibility of eternal happiness to heathens: because whatsoever is obscure is concluded not necessary to be known.

But by asserting the Scripture to be the canon of our faith, I have unavoidably created to myself two sorts of enemies: the Papists, indeed, more directly, because they have kept the Scripture from us what they could and have reserved to themselves a right of interpreting what they have delivered under the pretence of infallibility: and the Fanatics more collaterally, because they have assumed what amounts to an infallibility in the private spirit, and have detorted those texts of

Scripture which are not necessary to salvation to the damnable uses of sedition, disturbance, and destruction of the civil government. To begin with the Papists, and to speak freely, I think them the less dangerous, at least in appearance, to our present state, for not only the penal laws are in force against them, and their number is contemptible; but also their peerage and commons are excluded from parliaments, and consequently those laws in no probability of being repealed. A general and uninterrupted plot of their clergy ever since the Reformation I suppose all Protestants believe; for 'tis not reasonable to think but that so many of their orders, as were outed from their fat possessions, would endeavour a re-entrance against those whom they account heretics. As for the late design, Mr. Coleman's letters, for aught I know, are the best evidence; and what they discover, without wire-drawing their sense or malicious glosses, all men of reason conclude credible. If there be anything more than this required of me, I must believe it as well as I am able, in spite of the witnesses, and out of a decent conformity to the votes of Parliament; for I suppose the Fanatics will not allow the private spirit in this case. Here the infallibility is at least in one part of the government; and our understandings as well as our wills are represented. But to return to the

Roman Catholics, how can we be secure from the practice of Jesuited Papists in that religion? For not two or three of that order, as some of them would impose upon us, but almost the whole body of them are of opinion, that their infallible master has a right over kings, not only in spirituals but temporals. Not to name Mariana, Bellarmine, Emanuel Sa, Molina, Santarel, Simancha, and at least twenty others of foreign countries; we can produce of our own nation, Campion, and Doleman or Parsons: besides many are named whom I have not read, who all of them attest this doctrine, that the Pope can depose and give away the right of any sovereign prince, 'si vel paulum deflexerit,' if he shall never so little warp: but if he once comes to be excommunicated, then the bond of obedience is taken off from subjects; and they may and ought to drive him like another Nebuchadnezzar, ' ex hominum Christianorum dominatu,' from exercising dominion over Christians; and to this they are bound by virtue of divine precept, and by all the ties of conscience, under no less penalty than damnation. If they answer me, as a learned priest has lately written, that this doctrine of the Jesuits is not ' de fide,' and that consequently they are not obliged by it, they must pardon me if I think they have said nothing to the purpose; for 'tis a maxim in their Church, where points

of faith are not decided, and that doctors are
of contrary opinions, they may follow which
part they please; but more safely the most
received and most authorised. And their
champion Bellarmine has told the world, in
his Apology, that the King of England is a
vassal to the Pope 'ratione directi domini,'
and that he holds in villanage of his Roman
landlord. Which is no new claim put in for
England. Our chronicles are his authentic
witnesses, that King John was deposed by
the same plea, and Philip Augustus admitted
tenant. And which makes the more for
Bellarmine, the French King was again
ejected when our King submitted to the
Church, and the crown received under the
sordid condition of a vassalage.

'Tis not sufficient for the more moderate
and well-meaning Papists (of which I doubt
not there are many) to produce the evidences
of their loyalty to the late King, and to
declare their innocency in this Plot: I will
grant their behaviour in the first to have
been as loyal and as brave as they desire,
and will be willing to hold them excused as
to the second (I mean, when it comes to my
turn and after my betters, for it is a madness
to be sober alone, while the nation continues
drunk): but that saying of their Father Cres,
is still running in my head, that they may be
dispensed with in their obedience to an heretic
prince, while the necessity of the times shall

oblige them to it; for that, as another of
them tells us, is only the effect of Christian
prudence; but when once they shall get
power to shake him off, an heretic is no
lawful king, and consequently to rise against
him is no rebellion. I should be glad, therefore, that they would follow the advice which
was charitably given them by a reverend
prelate of our church; namely, that they
would join in a public act of disowning and
detesting those Jesuitic principles, and subscribe to all doctrines which deny the Pope's
authority of deposing kings, and releasing
subjects from their oath of allegiance; to
which I should think they might easily be
induced, if it be true that this present Pope
has condemned the doctrine of king-killing
(a thesis of the Jesuits) amongst others,
'ex cathedrâ,' as they call it, or in open
consistory.

Leaving them, therefore, in so fair a way
(if they please themselves) of satisfying all
reasonable men of their sincerity and good
meaning to the government, I shall make
bold to consider that other extreme of our
religion, I mean the Fanatics or Schismatics
of the English Church. Since the Bible has
been translated into our tongue, they have
used it so as if their business was not to be
saved, but to be damned by its contents. If
we consider only them, better had it been
for the English nation that it had still

remained in the original Greek and Hebrew, or at least in the honest Latin of St. Jerome, than that several texts in it should have been prevaricated to the destruction of that government which put it into so ungrateful hands.

How many heresies the first translation of Tyndal produced in few years, let my Lord Herbert's 'History of Henry the Eighth' inform you; insomuch that for the gross errors in it, and the great mischiefs it occasioned, a sentence passed on the first edition of the Bible, too shameful almost to be repeated. After the short reign of Edward the Sixth, who had continued to carry on the Reformation on other principles than it was begun, every one knows that not only the chief promoters of that work, but many other, whose consciences would not dispense with Popery, were forced for fear of persecution to change climates; from whence returning at the beginning of Queen Elizabeth's reign, many of them who had been in France and at Geneva brought back the rigid opinions and imperious discipline of Calvin, to graff upon our Reformation; which, though they cunningly concealed at first, as well knowing how nauseously that drug would go down in a lawful monarchy which was prescribed for a rebellious commonwealth, yet they always kept it in reserve, and were never wanting to themselves, either in court or parliament, when either they had any prospect of a numerous party of fanatic members in the one, or the encouragement of any favourite in the other, whose covetousness was gaping at the patrimony of the Church. They who will consult the works of our venerable Hooker, or the account of his life, or more particularly the letter written to him on this subject by George Cranmer, may see by what gradations they proceeded; from the dislike of cap and surplice, the very next step was admonitions to the parliament against the whole government ecclesiastical; then came out volumes in English and Latin in defence of their tenets; and immediately practices were set on foot to erect their discipline without authority. Those not succeeding, satire and railing was the next; and Martin Mar-prelate, the Marvel of those times, was the first presbyterian scribbler who sanctified libels and scurrility to the use of the good old cause. Which was done, says my author, upon this account: that, their serious treatises having been fully answered and refuted, they might compass by railing what they had lost by reasoning; and, when their cause was sunk in court and parliament, they might at least hedge in a stake amongst the rabble; for to their ignorance all things are wit which are abusive; but if Church and State were made the theme, then the doctoral degree of wit

82

was to be taken at Billingsgate ; even the
most saint-like of the party, though they
durst not excuse this contempt and vilifying
of the government, yet were pleased, and
grinned at it with a pious smile, and called
it a judgment of God against the hierarchy.
Thus sectaries, we may see, were born
with teeth, foul-mouthed and scurrilous from
their infancy ; and if spiritual pride, venom,
violence, contempt of superiors, and slander,
had been the marks of orthodox belief, the
Presbytery and the rest of our Schismatics,
which are their spawn, were always the most
visible Church in the Christian world.

'Tis true, the government was too strong
at that time for a rebellion ; but to show
what proficiency they had made in Calvin's
school, even then their mouths watered at
it ; for two of their gifted brotherhood,
Hacket and Coppinger, as the story tells us,
got up into a pease-cart and harangued the
people, to dispose them to an insurrection
and to establish their discipline by force; so
that, however it comes about that now they
celebrate Queen Elizabeth's birthnight, as
that of their saint, and patroness, yet then
they were for doing the work of the Lord
by arms against her ; and in all probability
they wanted but a fanatic lord-mayor and
two sheriffs of their party to have compassed it.

Our venerable Hooker, after many ad-

monitions which he had given them, towards
the end of his preface breaks out into this
prophetic speech: 'There is in every one
of these considerations most just cause to
fear, lest our hastiness to embrace a thing
of so perilous consequence, [meaning the
Presbyterian discipline,] should cause posterity
to feel those evils which as yet are more easy
for us to prevent than they would be for them
to remedy.'

How fatally this Cassandra has foretold,
we know too well by sad experience: the
seeds were sown in the time of Queen
Elizabeth, the bloody harvest ripened in the
reign of King Charles the Martyr; and,
because all the sheaves could not be carried
off without shedding some of the loose
grains, another crop is too likely to follow;
nay, I fear 'tis unavoidable, if the Conven-
ticlers be permitted still to scatter.

A man may be suffered to quote an
adversary to our religion, when he speaks
truth. And 'tis the observation of Maim-
bourg, in his 'History of Calvinism,' that
wherever that discipline was planted and
embraced, rebellion, civil war, and misery
attended it. And how, indeed, should it
happen otherwise; Reformation of Church
and State has always been the ground of
our divisions in England. While we were
Papists, our holy Father rid us by pretending
authority out of the Scriptures to depose

princes; when we shook off his authority, the sectaries furnished themselves with the same weapons, and out of the same magazine, the Bible: so that the Scriptures, which are in themselves the greatest security of governors, as commanding express obedience to them, are now turned to their destruction: and never, since the Reformation, has there wanted a text of their interpreting to authorise a rebel. And 'tis to be noted, by the way, that the doctrines of king-killing and deposing, which have been taken up only by the worst party of the Papists, the most frontless flatterers of the Pope's authority, have been espoused, defended, and are still maintained by the whole body of Nonconformists and Republicans. 'Tis but dubbing themselves the people of God, which 'tis the interest of their preachers to tell them they are, and their own interest to believe; and, after that, they cannot dip into the Bible, but one text or another will turn up for their purpose: if they are under persecution, as they call it, then that is a mark of their election; if they flourish, then God works miracles for their deliverance, and the saints are to possess the earth.

They may think themselves to be too roughly handled in this paper; but I, who know best how far I could have gone on this subject, must be bold to tell them they are spared: though at the same time I am not ignorant that they interpret the mildness of a writer to them, as they do the mercy of the government; in the one they think it fear, and conclude it weakness in the other. The best way for them to confute me is, as I before advised the Papists, to disclaim their principles and renounce their practices. We shall all be glad to think them true Englishmen, when they obey the King: and true Protestants, when they conform to the Church discipline.

It remains that I acquaint the reader, that the verses were written for an ingenious young gentleman, my friend, upon his Translation of 'The Critical History of the Old Testament,' composed by the learned Father Simon: the verses therefore are addressed to the translator of that work, and the style of them is, what it ought to be, epistolary.

If any one be so lamentable a critic as to require the smoothness, the numbers, and the turn of heroic poetry in this poem, I must tell him, that, if he has not read Horace, I have studied him, and hope the style of his Epistles is not ill imitated here. The expressions of a poem designed purely for instruction ought to be plain and natural, and yet majestic: for here the poet is presumed to be a kind of lawgiver, and those three qualities which I have named are proper to the legislative style. The florid, elevated, and figurative way is for the passions ; for love and hatred, fear and anger, are begotten in the soul by showing their objects out of their true proportion, either greater than the life or less ; but instruction is to be given by showing them what they naturally are. A man is to be cheated into passion, but to be reasoned into truth.

ROGER L'ESTRANGE

TRANSLATIONS OF ÆSOP'S FABLES

Fable 4.—A FROG AND A MOUSE

There fell out a bloody quarrel once betwixt
the frogs and the mice, about the sovereignty
of the fens ; and whilst two of their champions
were disputing it at sword's point, down
comes a kite powdering upon them in the
interim, and gobbles up both together, to
part the fray.

Fable 5.—A LION AND A BEAR

There was a lion and a bear had gotten a
fawn betwixt them, and there were they at
it tooth and nail, which of the two should
carry 't off. They fought it out, till they were
e'en glad to lie down and take breath. In
which instant a fox passing that way, and
finding how the case stood with the two
combatants, seized upon the fawn for his
own use, and so very fairly scampered away
with him. The lion and the bear saw the
whole action, but not being in condition to
rise and hinder it, they passed this reflection

ROGER L'ESTRANGE

upon the whole matter: Here have we been
worrying one another who should have the
booty, till this cursed fox has robbed us both
on 't.

The Moral of the two Fables above

'Tis the fate of all Gotham quarrels, when
fools go together by the ears, to have knaves
run away with the stakes.

Reflection

This is no more than what we see daily
in popular factions, where pragmatical fools
commonly begin the squabble, and crafty
knaves reap the benefit of it. There is very
rarely any quarrel, either public or private,
whether betwixt persons or parties, but a
third watches and hopes to be the better
for 't.

And all is but according to the old proverb:
While two dogs are fighting for a bone, a
third runs away with it. Divide and govern
is a rule of state that we see confirmed and
supported by daily practice and experience;
so that 'tis none of the slightest arguments
for the necessity of a common peace, that the
litigants tear one another to pieces for the
benefit of some third interest that takes advantage of their disagreement. This is no
more than what we find upon experience
through the whole history of the world in
all notable changes and revolutions; that is

to say, the contendents have still been made a prey to a third party. And this has been not only the fate and the event of popular quarrels, but the punishment of them; for the judgment still treads upon the heel of the wickedness. People may talk of liberty, property, conscience, right of title, etc., but the main business and earnest of the world is money, dominion, and power, and how to compass those ends; and not a rush matter at last, whether it be by force or by cunning. Might and right are inseparable in the opinion of the world; and he that has the longer sword shall never want either lawyers or divines to defend his claim. But then comes the kite or the fox in the conclusion; that is to say, some third party, that either by strength or by craft, masters both plaintiff and defendant and carries away the booty.

Fable 19.—THE FROGS CHOOSE A KING

In the days of old, when the frogs were all at liberty in the lakes, and grown quite weary of living without government, they petitioned Jupiter for a king, to the end that there might be some distinction of good and evil, by certain equitable rules and methods of rewards and punishment. Jupiter, that knew the vanity of their hearts, threw them down a log for their governor, which upon the first dash frighted the whole mobile of them into the mud for the very fear on 't. This panic terror kept them in awe for a while, till in good time one frog, bolder than the rest, put up his head and looked about him, to see how squares went with their new king. Upon this he calls his fellow-subjects together; opens the truth of the case, and nothing would serve them then but riding a top of him, insomuch that the dread they were in before is now turned into insolence and tumult. This king, they said, was too tame for them, and Jupiter must needs be entreated to send 'em another. He did so. But authors are divided upon it, whether 'twas a stork or a serpent, though whether of the two soever it was, he left them neither liberty nor property, but made a prey of his subjects. Such was their condition, in fine, that they sent Mercury to Jupiter yet once again for another king, whose answer was this: They that will not be contented when they are well, must be patient when things are amiss with them; and people had better rest where they are, than go farther and fare worse.

The Moral

The mobile are uneasy without a ruler; they are as restless with one; and the oftener they shift, the worse they are. So that government, or no government; a king of God's making, or of the people's, or none at all—the multitude are never to be satisfied.

ROGER L'ESTRANGE

Reflection

This fable, under the emblem of the frogs,
sets forth the murmuring and the unsteadi-
ness of the common people; that in a state
of liberty will have a king. They do not like
him when they have him, and so change
again, and grow sicker of the next than they
were of the former. Now the business is
only this: they are never satisfied with their
present condition, but their governors are
still either too dull, or too rigid. 'Tis a
madness for him that is free to put himself
into a state of bondage, and rather than bear
a less misfortune to hazard a greater.

This allusion of the frogs runs upon all four
(as they say) in the resemblance of the multitude, both for the humour, the murmur, the
importunity, and the subject-matter of the
petition. Redress of grievances is the question, and the devil of it is, that the petitioners
are never to be pleased. In one fit they
cannot be without government; in another
they cannot bear the yoke on't. They find
absolute freedom to be a direct state of war;
for where there's no means of either preventing strife, or ending it, the weaker are
still a prey to the stronger. One king is too
soft and easy for them; another too fierce!
And then a third change would do better,
they think. Now, 'tis impossible to satisfy
people that would have they know not what.

92

They beg, and wrangle, and appeal, and
their answer is at last, that if they shift again
they shall be still worse; by which the frogs
are given to understand the very truth of the
matter, as we find it in the world, both in the
nature and reason of the thing, and in policy
and religion: which is, that kings are from
God, and that it is a sin, a folly, and a madness, to struggle with His appointments.

Fable 37

There was an old, hungry lion would fain
have been dealing with a piece of good horse-
flesh that he had in his eye; but the nag he
thought would be too fleet for him, unless he
could supply the want of heels by artifice and
address. He puts himself into the garb and
habit of a professor of physic, and according
to the humour of the world, sets up for a
doctor of the college.

Under this pretext, he lets fall a word or
two by way of discourse upon the subject of
his trade; but the horse smelt him out, and
presently a crotchet came in his head how he
might countermine him. 'I got a thorn in
my foot the other day,' says the horse, 'as I
was crossing a thicket, and I am e'en quite
lame on 't.'—'Oh,' says the new physician,
'do but hold up your leg a little, and I will
cure you immediately.' The lion presently
puts himself in posture for the office; but the

patient was too nimble for his doctor, and
so soon as ever he had him fair for his purpose, gave him so terrible a rebuke upon the
forehead with his heel, that he laid him at
his length, and so got off with a whole skin,
before the other could execute his design.

The Moral of the two Fables above

Harm watch, harm catch, is but according
to the common rule of equity and retaliation,
and a very warrantable way of deceiving the
deceiver.

Reflection

There's no trusting to the fair words of those
that have both an interest and an inclination
to destroy us; especially when the design is
carried on under the mask of a friendly office.
It is but reasonable to oppose art to art, and
where we suspect false play to encounter one
trick with another: provided always that it be
managed without breach of faith, and within
the compass of honour, honesty and good
manners. The wolf had the same design upon
the ass that the lion had upon the horse; and
the matter being only brought to a trial of
skill between them, the countermine was only
an act of self-preservation.

Fable 68.—A DOG AND A WOLF

There was a hagged carrion of a wolf, and
a jolly sort of a gentile dog, with good flesh

94

upon his back, that fell into company together upon the king's highway. The wolf wonderfully pleased with his companion, and as inquisitive to learn how he brought himself to that blessed state of body.

Why, says the dog, I keep my master's house from thieves and I have very good meat, drink, and lodging for my pains. Now if you'll go along with me, and do as I do, you may fare as I fare. The wolf struck up the bargain, and so away they trotted together. But as they were jogging on, the wolf spied a bare place about the Dog's neck, where the hair was worn off. Brother, (says he), how comes this, I pr'y thee? Oh, that's nothing, says the dog, but the fretting of my collar a little. Nay, says t'other, if there be a collar in the case, I know better things than to sell my liberty for a crust.

Reflection

In this emblem is set forth the blessing of liberty, and the sordid meaning of those wretches that sacrifice their freedom to their lusts, and their palates. What man in his right senses, that has wherewithal to live free, would make himself a slave for superfluities. The wolf would have been well enough content to have bartered away a ragged coat, and a raw-boned carcass, for a smooth and a fat one; but when they came to talk of a collar

95

once, away marches he to his own trade in the woods again, and makes the better choice of the two.

Fable 75

An eagle made a stoop at a lamb ; truss'd it, and took it cleverly away with her. A mimical daw, that saw this exploit, would needs try the same experiment upon a ram : but his claws were so shackled in the fleece with hugging to get him up, that the shepherd came in, and caught him, before he could clear himself. He clipped his wings, and carried him home to his children to play withal. They came gaping about him, and asked their father what strange bird that was? Why, says he, he'll tell you himself that he's an eagle ; but if you'll take my word for't, I know him to be a daw.

The Moral

'Tis a high degree of vanity and folly, for men to take more upon them than they are able to go through withal ; and the end of those undertakings is only mockery and disappointment in the conclusion.

Reflection

'Tis vain and dangerous to enter into competitions with our superiors, in what kind

soever, whether it be in arms, letters, expense,
strength of body, arts and sciences or the
like. 'Tis impossible for any man, in fine, to
take a true measure of another without an
exact knowledge, and a true judgment of himself. Nay, the attempt of anything above
our force with vanity and presumption, most
certainly ends in a miscarriage that makes
the pretender ridiculous. The outdoing of a
great man in his own way, saviour in some
degree of ill-manners, as it is upon the main,
a high point of indiscretion. One man takes
it for an affront to be outwitted ; another to be
out-fooled, as Nero could not endure to be out-
fiddled. But in short, be the matter never so
great, or never so trivial, 'tis the same case as
to the envy of the competition.

Fable 174

A wolf spied out a straggling kid, and pur-
sued him. The kid found that the wolf was too
nimble for him, and so turned and told him ;
I perceive I am to be eaten, and I would
gladly die as pleasantly as I could : wherefore
pray give me but one touch of your pipe before
I go to pot. The wolf played, and the kid
danced, and the noise of the pipe brought in
the dogs upon him. Well (says the wolf) thus
'tis when people will be meddling out of their
profession. My business was to play the
butcher, not the piper.

ROGER L'ESTRANGE

The Moral

When a crafty knave is infatuated, any
silly wretch may put tricks upon him.

Reflection

Let every man stick to his own part, without taking another man's trade out of his hand.
This is the old moral, but we may read upon't
another way too. 'Tis a very unequal encounter, when malice, craft, and power are
united against the weak and the innocent:
saving where providence interposes to the
relief of the one, and to the infatuation of the
other: as the wolf here, that had a plot upon
the kid, was confounded by a counter-plot of
the kid upon the wolf, and such a counter-
plot it was too, as the wolf with all his
sagacity was not able to smell out. Wherefore let no man presume too much upon his
own strength, either of body or of mind; but
consider within himself, that heaven takes
part with the oppressed; and that tyrants
themselves are upon their behaviour to a
superior power.

Fable 294

Why don't you run and make haste? cried
the timber in a cart, to the oxen that drew it?
The burden is not so heavy sure. Well, (said
the oxen) if you did but know your own

fortune, you'd never be so merry at ours. We shall be discharged of our load so soon as we come to our journey's end, but you that are designed for beams and supporters shall be made to bear till your hearts break. This hint brought the timber to a better understanding of the case.

The Moral

'Tis matter of humanity, honour, prudence, and piety, to be tender one of another; for no man living knows his end, and 'tis the evening crowns the day.

Reflection

It is both base and foolish to insult over people in distress, for the wheel of fortune is perpetually in motion, and he that 's uppermost to-day, may be under it to-morrow. No man knows what end he is born to; and it is only death that can pronounce upon a happy or a miserable life. When the timber made sport with the oxen for the drudgery they laboured under, little did they dream of the greater oppression they were to undergo themselves.

EARL OF SHAFTESBURY

FROM AN ESSAY ON THE FREEDOM
OF WIT AND HUMOUR

I have been considering (my friend) what
your fancy was, to express such a surprise as
you did the other day, when I happened to
speak to you in commendation of raillery.
Was it possible you should suppose me so
grave a man, as to dislike all conversation of
this kind? Or were you afraid I should not
stand the trial, if you put me to it, by making
the experiment in my own case?

I must confess, you had reason enough for
your caution; if you could imagine me at the
bottom so true a zealot as not to bear the least
raillery on my own opinions. 'Tis the case,
I know, with many. Whatever they think
grave or solemn, they suppose must never
be treated out of a grave and solemn way:
though what another thinks they can be
contented to treat otherwise; and are forward
to try the edge of ridicule against any opinions
besides their own.

The question is, whether this be fair or no,
and whether it be not just and reasonable, to

make as free with our own opinions as with those of other people? For to be sparing in this case, may be looked upon as a piece of selfishness. We may be charged perhaps with wilful ignorance and blind idolatry, for having taken opinions upon trust, and consecrated in ourselves certain idol notions which we will never suffer to be unveiled or seen in open light. They may perhaps be monsters, and not divinities or sacred truths, which are kept thus choicely in some dark corner of our minds: the spectres may impose on us, whilst we refuse to turn 'em every way, and view their shapes and complexions in every light. For that which can be shown only in a certain light is questionable. Truth, 'tis supposed, may bear all lights: and one of these principal lights or natural mediums, by which things are to be viewed, in order to a thorough recognition, is ridicule itself, or that manner of proof by which we discern whatever is liable to just raillery in any subject. So much, at least, is allowed by all who at any time appeal to this criterion. The gravest gentlemen, even in the gravest subjects, are supposed to acknowledge this: and can have no right, 'tis thought, to deny others the freedom of this appeal; whilst they are free to censure like other men, and in their gravest arguments make no scruple to ask, is it not ridiculous?

Of this affair, therefore, I design you should

know fully what my sentiments are. And by this means you will be able to judge of me; whether I was sincere the other day in the defence of raillery, and can continue still to plead for those ingenious friends of ours who are often censured for their humour of this kind, and for the freedom they take in such an airy way of conversation and writing.

In good earnest, when one considers what use is sometimes made of this species of Wit, and to what an excess it has risen of late, in some characters of the age; one may be startled a little, and in doubt what to think of the practice, or whither this rallying humour will at length carry us. It has passed from the men of pleasure to the men of business. Politicians have been infected with it; and the grave affairs of state have been treated with an air of irony and banter. The ablest negotiators have been known the notablest buffoons; the most celebrated authors, the greatest masters of Burlesque.

There is, indeed, a kind of defensive raillery (if I may so call it) which I am willing enough to allow in affairs of whatever kind; when the spirit of curiosity would force a discovery of more truth than can conveniently be told. For we can never do more injury to truth, than by discovering too much of it, on some occasions. 'Tis the same with understandings as with eyes. To such a certain size and make just so much light is necessary, and no more. Whatever is beyond, brings darkness and confusion.

'Tis real humanity and kindness, to hide strong truths from tender eyes. And to do this by a pleasant amusement, is easier, and civiller, than by a hard denial, or remarkable reserve. But to go about industriously to confound men, in a mysterious manner, and to make advantage, or draw pleasure, from that perplexity they are thrown into, by such uncertain talk; is as unhandsome in a way of raillery, as when done with the greatest seriousness, or in the most solemn way of deceit. It may be necessary, as well now as heretofore, for wise men to speak in parables, and with a double meaning, that the enemy may be amused, and they only who have ears to hear, may hear. But 'tis certainly a mean, impotent, and dull sort of wit, which amuses all alike, and leaves the most sensible man, and even a friend, equally in doubt, and at a loss to understand what one's real mind is, upon any subject.

This is that gross sort of raillery, which is so offensive in good company. And indeed there is as much difference between one sort and another, as between fair dealing and hypocrisy; or between the genteelest wit, and the most scurrilous buffoonery. But by freedom of conversation this liberal kind of wit will lose its credit. For wit is its own remedy. Liberty and commerce bring it to its true

standard. The only danger is, the laying
of an embargo. The same thing happens here
as in the case of trade. Impositions and re-
strictions reduce it to a low ebb : nothing is so
advantageous to it as a free post.
We have seen in our own time the decline
and ruin of a false sort of wit, which so much
delighted our ancestors, that their poems and
plays, as well as sermons, were full of it. All
humour had something of the quibble. The
very language of the court was punning. But
'tis now banished the town, and all good
company : there are only some few footsteps
of it in the country : and it seems at last confined to the nurseries of youth, as the chief
entertainment of pedants, and their pupils.
And thus, in other respects wit will mend upon
our hands, and humour will refine itself ; if we
take care not to tamper with it and bring it
under constraint, by severe usage and rigorous
prescriptions. All politeness is owing to
liberty. We polish one another, and rub off
our corners and rough sides by a sort of ami-
cable collision. To restrain this, is inevitably
to bring a rust upon men's understandings.
'Tis a destroying of civility, good-breeding,
and even charity itself, under pretence of main-
taining it.

ADVICE TO AN AUTHOR

'Tis easy to imagine, that amidst the several styles and manners of discourse or writing, the easiest attained, and earliest practised, was the miraculous, the pompous, or what we generally call the sublime. Astonishment is of all other passions the easiest raised in raw and unexperienced mankind. Children in their earliest infancy are entertained in this manner ; and the known way of pleasing such as these, is to make 'em wonder, and lead the way for 'em in this passion, by a feigned surprise at the miraculous objects we set before 'em. The best music of Barbarians is hideous and astonishing sounds. And the fine sights of Indians are enormous figures, various odd and glaring colours, and whatever of that sort is amazingly beheld, with a kind of horror and consternation.

In poetry and studied prose, the astonishing part or what commonly passes for sublime, is formed by the variety of figures, the multiplicity of metaphors, and by quitting as much as possible the natural and easy way of expression, for that which is most unlike to humanity, or ordinary uses. This the Prince of Critics assures us to have been the manner of the earliest poets, before the age of Homer; or till such time as this father-poet came into repute, who deposed that spurious race, and gave rise to a legitimate and genuine kind. He retained only what was decent of the figurative or metaphoric style, introduced the natural and simple : and turned his thoughts towards the real beauty of composition, the unity of design, the truth of characters, and the just imitation of nature in each particular.

The manner of this father-poet was afterwards variously imitated, and divided into several shares ; especially when it came to be copied in dramatic. Tragedy came first ; and took what was most solemn and sublime. In this part the poets succeeded sooner than in comedy or the facetious kind ; as was natural indeed to suppose, since this was in reality the easiest manner of the two, and capable of being brought the soonest to perfection. For so the same Prince of Critics sufficiently informs us. And 'tis highly worth remarking, what this mighty genius and judge of art declares concerning tragedy ; that whatever idea might be formed of the utmost perfection of this kind of poem, it could in practice rise no higher than it had been already carried in his time. ' Having at length (says he) attained its ends, and being apparently consummate in itself.' But for comedy, it seems, 'twas still in hand. It had been already in some manner reduced : but, as he plainly insinuates, it lay yet unfinished ; notwithstanding the witty labours of an Aristophanes, and the other comic poets of the first manner, who had flourished

a whole age before this critic. As perfect as
were those wits in style and language ; and
as fertile in all the varieties and turns of
humour ; yet the truth of characters, the beauty
of order, and the simple imitation of nature
were in a manner wholly unknown to 'em ; or
through petulancy, or debauch of humour,
were, it seems, neglected and set aside. A
Menander had not as yet appeared ; who arose
soon after, to accomplish the prophecy of our
grand Master of Art, ar#d consummate Philo-
logist.

Comedy had at this time done little more
than what the ancient parodies had done
before it. 'Twas of admirable use to explode
the false sublime of early poets, and such as in
its own age were on every occasion ready to
relapse into that vicious manner. The good
tragedians themselves could hardly escape its
lashes. The pompous orators were its never-
failing subjects. Everything which might be
imposing, by a false gravity or solemnity, was
forced to endure the trial of this touchstone.
Manners and characters as well as speech and
writings were discussed with the greatest
freedom. Nothing could be better fitted than
this genius of wit to unmask the face of things,
and remove those larvae naturally formed
from the tragic manner, and pompous style
which had preceded :

Et docuit magnumque loci, nitique Cothurno,
Sucessit vetus his Comoedia.

JOSEPH ADDISON AND
RICHARD STEELE

JOSEPH ADDISON

'Non fumum ex fulgore, sed ex fumo dare
    lucem
Cogitat, ut speciosa dehinc miracula promat.'
                                        Hor.

I have observed that a reader seldom peruses
a book with pleasure, till he knows whether
the writer of it be a black or a fair man, of
a mild or choleric disposition, married or a
bachelor, with other particulars of the like
nature, that conduce very much to the right
understanding of an author. To gratify this
curiosity, which is so natural to a reader,
I design this paper and my next as prefatory
discourses to my following writings, and shall
give some account in them of the several
persons that are engaged in this work. As
the chief trouble of compiling, digesting, and
correcting, will fall to my share, I must do
myself the justice to open the work with my
own history.

I was born to a small hereditary estate,
which, according to the tradition of the vil-

lage where it lies, was bounded by the same
hedges and ditches in William the Con-
queror's time that it is at present, and has
been delivered down from father to son,
whole and entire, without the loss or acqui-
sition of a single field or meadow during the
space of six hundred years. There runs a
story in the family that, about six months
before I was born, my mother dreamt that
she had given birth to a judge. Whether
this might proceed from a lawsuit which was
then depending in the family, or my father's
being a justice of the peace, I cannot determine; for I am not so vain as to think it
presaged any dignity that I should arrive at
in my future life, though that was the interpretation which the neighbourhood put upon
it. The gravity of my behaviour at my very
first appearance in the world, and all the time
that I sucked, seemed to favour my mother's
dream, for, as she has often told me, I threw
away my rattle before I was two months
old, and would not make use of my coral until
they had taken away the bells from it.

As for the rest of my infancy, there being
nothing in it remarkable, I shall pass it over
in silence. I find that during my nonage I
had the reputation of a very sullen youth,
but was always a favourite with my school-
master, who used to say that ' my parts were
solid, and would wear well.' I had not been
long at the university before I distinguished

myself by the most profound silence; for
during the space of eight years, excepting
in the public exercises of the college, I scarce
uttered the quantity of a hundred words, and
indeed do not remember that I ever spoke
three sentences together in my whole life.
Whilst I was in this learned body, I applied
myself with so much diligence to my studies,
that there are very few celebrated books,
either in the learned or the modern tongues,
which I am not acquainted with.

Upon the death of my father, I was resolved
to travel into foreign countries, and therefore
left the university with the character of an
odd unaccountable fellow, that had a great
deal of learning if he would but show it. An
insatiable thirst after knowledge carried me
into all the countries of Europe, in which
there was anything new or strange to be
seen; nay, to such a degree was my curiosity
raised, that, having read the controversies
of some great men concerning the antiquities
of Egypt, I made a voyage to Grand Cairo
on purpose to take the measure of a pyramid;
and, as soon as I had set myself right in that
particular, returned to my native country with
great satisfaction.

I have passed my latter years in this city,
where I am frequently seen in most public
places, though there are not above half a
dozen of my select friends that know me;
of whom my next paper shall give a more

particular account. There is no place of general resort wherein I do not often make my appearance. Sometimes I am seen thrusting my head into a round of politicians at Will's, and listening with great attention to the narratives that are made in those little circular audiences. Sometimes I smoke a pipe at Child's; and, whilst I seem attentive to nothing but the postman, overhear the conversation of every table in the room. I appear on Sunday nights at St. James's coffee-house, and sometimes join the little committee of politics in the inner room, as one who comes there to hear and improve. My face is likewise very well known at the Grecian, the Cocoa-tree, and in the theatres both of Drury-lane and the Haymarket. I have been taken for a merchant upon the Exchange for above these ten years, and sometimes pass for a Jew in the assembly of stockjobbers at Jonathan's. In short, wherever I see a cluster of people, I always mix with them, though I never open my lips but in my own club.

Thus I live in the world rather as a spectator of mankind than as one of the species, by which means I have made myself a speculative statesman, soldier, merchant, and artisan, without ever meddling with any practical part of life. I am very well versed in the theory in a husband, or a father, and can discern the errors in the economy, business, and diversion

III

of others, better than those who are engaged
in them ; as standers-by discover blots which
are apt to escape those who are in the game.
I never espoused any party with violence,
and am resolved to observe an exact neu-
trality between the Whigs and Tories, unless
I shall be forced to declare myself by the
hostilities of either side. In short, I have
acted in all the parts of my life as a looker-
on, which is the character I intend to preserve in this paper.

I have given the reader just so much of my
history and character as to let him see I am
not altogether unqualified for the business I
have undertaken. As for other particulars
in my life and adventures, I shall insert them
in following papers, as I shall see occasion.
In the mean time, when I consider how much I
have seen, read, and heard, I begin to blame my
own taciturnity ; and, since I have neither time
nor inclination to communicate the fulness of
my heart in speech, I am resolved to do it in
writing, and to print myself out, if possible,
before I die. I have been often told by my
friends that it is a pity so many useful discoveries which I have made should be in the
possession of a silent man. For this reason,
therefore, I shall publish a sheet full of
thoughts every morning for the benefit of
my contemporaries ; and if I can any way
contribute to the diversion or improvement
of the country in which I live, I shall leave

JOSEPH ADDISON

it, when I am summoned out of it, with the
secret satisfaction of thinking that I have not
lived in vain.

There are three very material points which
I have not spoken to in this paper, and which,
for several important reasons, I must keep to
myself, at least for some time: I mean, an
account of my name, my age, and my lodgings.
I must confess I would gratify my reader in
anything that is reasonable; but as for these
three particulars, though I am sensible they
might tend very much to the embellishment
of my paper, I cannot yet come to a resolution
of communicating them to the public. They
would indeed draw me out of that obscurity
which I have enjoyed for many years, and expose me in public places to several salutes and
civilities which have been always very disagreeable to me; for the greatest pain I can
suffer is the being talked to, and being stared
at. It is for this reason, likewise, that I
keep my complexion and dress as very great
secrets; though it is not impossible but that
I may make discoveries of both in the pro-
gress of the work I have undertaken.

After having been thus particular upon
myself, I shall in to-morrow's paper give an
account of those gentlemen who are concerned
with me in this work; for, as I have before
intimated, a plan of it is laid and concerted
(as all other matters of importance are) in a
club. However, as my friends have engaged

me to stand in the front, those who have a mind to correspond with me may direct their letters to the 'Spectator,' at Mr. Buckley's in Little Britain. For I must further acquaint the reader, that though our club meets only on Tuesdays and Thursdays, we have appointed a committee to sit every night for the inspection of all such papers as may contribute to the advancement of the public weal.

RICHARD STEELE

'. . . Ast alii sex
Et plures uno conclamant ore. . .'
Juv.

The first of our society is a gentleman of Worcestershire, of ancient descent, a baronet, his name Sir Roger de Coverley. His great grandfather was inventor of that famous country dance which is called after him. All who know that shire are very well acquainted with the parts and merits of Sir Roger. He is a gentleman that is very singular in his behaviour, but his singularities proceed from his good sense, and are contradictions to the manners of the world, only as he thinks the world is in the wrong. However, this humour creates him no enemies, for he does nothing with sourness or obstinacy; and his being

unconfined to modes and forms make him
but the readier and more capable to please
and oblige all who know him. When he is
in town, he lives in Soho Square. It is said
he keeps himself a bachelor by reason he was
crossed in love by a perverse beautiful widow
of the next county to him. Before this disappointment Sir Roger was what you call
a fine gentleman, had often supped with my
Lord Rochester and Sir George Etherege,
fought a duel upon his first coming to town,
and kicked bully Dawson in a public coffee-
house for calling him 'youngster.' But being
ill-used by the above-mentioned widow, he
was very serious for a year and a half; and
though, his temper being naturally jovial, he
at last got over it, he grew careless of himself, and never dressed afterwards. He continues to wear a coat and doublet of the same
cut that were in fashion at the time of his
repulse, which, in his merry humours, he tells
us has been in and out twelve times since he
wore it. He is now in his fifty-sixth year,
cheerful, gay, and hearty; keeps a good
house both in town and country; a great
lover of mankind; but there is such a mirthful
cast in his behaviour that he is rather beloved
than esteemed.

His tenants grow rich, his servants look
satisfied, all the young women profess love to
him, and the young men are glad of his company. When he comes into a house, he calls

the servants by their names, and talks all the way upstairs to a visit. I must not omit that Sir Roger is a justice of the quorum; that he fills the chair at a quarter session with great abilities, and, three months ago, gained universal applause by explaining a passage in the Game Act.

The gentleman next in esteem and authority among us is another bachelor, who is a member of the Inner Temple, a man of great probity, wit, and understanding; but he has chosen his place of residence rather to obey the direction of an old humoursome father than in pursuit of his own inclinations. He was placed there to study the laws of the land, and is the most learned of any of the house in those of the stage. Aristotle and Longinus are much better understood by him than Littleton or Coke. The father sends up every post questions relating to marriage articles, leases, and tenures, in the neighbourhood; all which questions he agrees with an attorney to answer and take care of in the lump. He is studying the passions themselves, when he should be inquiring into the debates among men which arise from them. He knows the argument of each of the orations of Demosthenes and Tully, but not one case in the reports of our own courts. No one ever took him for a fool; but none, except his intimate friends, know he has a great deal of wit. This turn makes him at once both disinterested and agreeable. As few of his thoughts are drawn from business, they are most of them fit for conversation. His taste of books is a little too just for the age he lives in; he has read all, but approves of very few. His familiarity with the customs, manners, actions, and writings of the ancients, makes him a very delicate observer of what occurs to him in the present world. He is an excellent critic, and the time of the play is his hour of business: exactly at five he passes through New Inn, crosses through Russell Court, and takes a turn at Will's till the play begins: he has his shoes rubbed, and his periwig powdered at the barber's as you go into the Rose. It is for the good of the audience when he is at the play, for the actors have an ambition to please him.

The person of next consideration is Sir Andrew Freeport, a merchant of great eminence in the city of London: a person of indefatigable industry, strong reason, and great experience. His notions of trade are noble and generous, and (as every rich man has usually some sly way of jesting, which would make no great figure were he not a rich man) he calls the sea the British Common. He is acquainted with commerce in all its parts; and will tell you that it is a stupid and barbarous way to extend dominion by arms; for true power is to be got by arts

and industry. He will often argue that, if
this part of our trade were well cultivated,
we should gain from one nation ; and if
another, from another. I have heard him
prove that diligence makes more lasting acquisitions than valour, and that sloth has
ruined more nations than the sword. He
abounds in several frugal maxims, among
which the greatest favourite is, 'A penny
saved is a penny got.' A general trader of
good sense is pleasanter company than a
general scholar : and Sir Andrew, having a
natural unaffected eloquence, the perspicuity
of his discourse gives the same pleasure that
wit would in another man. He has made
his fortunes himself ; and says that England
may be richer than other kingdoms by as
plain methods as he himself is richer than
other men ; though at the same time I can
say this of him, that there is not a point
in the compass but blows home a ship in
which he is an owner.

Next to Sir Andrew in the club-room sits
Captain Sentry, a gentleman of great courage,
good understanding, but invincible modesty.
He is one of those that deserve very well,
but are very awkward at putting their talents
within the observation of such as should take
notice of them. He was some years a captain,
and behaved himself with great gallantry in
several engagements and at several sieges ;
but having a small estate of his own, and

being next heir to Sir Roger, he has quitted a way of life in which no man can rise suitably to his merit who is not something of a courtier as well as a soldier. I have heard him often lament that, in a profession where merit is placed in so conspicuous a view, impudence should get the better of modesty. When he has talked to this purpose, I never heard him make a sour expression, but frankly confess that he left the world because he was not fit for it. A strict honesty and an even regular behaviour are in themselves obstacles to him that must press through crowds, who endeavour at the same end with himself, the favour of a commander. He will, however, in his way of talk, excuse generals for not disposing according to men's desert, or inquiring into it; for, says he, that great man who has a mind to help me has as many to break through to come at me as I have to come at him: therefore, he will conclude, that the man who would make a figure, especially in a military way, must get over all false modesty, and assist his patron against the importunity of other pretenders, by a proper assurance in his own vindication. He says it is a civil cowardice to be backward in asserting what you ought to expect, as it is a military fear to be slow in attacking when it is your duty. With this candour does the gentleman speak of himself and others. The same frankness runs through all his conver-

sation. The military part of his life has furnished him with many adventures, in the
relation of which he is very agreeable to the
company; for he is never overbearing, though
accustomed to command men in the utmost
degree below him; nor ever too obsequious,
from a habit of obeying men highly above
him.

But that our society may not appear a set
of humorists, unacquainted with the gallantries and pleasantries of the age, we have
among us the gallant Will Honeycomb, a
gentleman who, according to his years,
should be in the decline of his life; but
having ever been very careful of his person,
and always had a very easy fortune, time
has made but very little impression, either
by wrinkles on his forehead or traces in his
brain. His person is well turned and of
good height. He is very ready at that sort
of discourse with which men usually entertain women. He has all his life dressed very
well; and remembers habits as others do
men. He can smile when one speaks to him,
and laughs easily. He knows the history of
every mode, and can inform you from what
Frenchwoman our wives and daughters had
this manner of curling their hair, that way
of placing their hoods; and whose vanity to
show her foot made that part of the dress
so short in such a year. In a word, all his
conversation and knowledge have been in

the female world. As other men of his age will take notice to you what such a minister said on such and such an occasion, he will tell you when the Duke of Monmouth danced at court, such a woman was then smitten, another was taken with him at the head of his troop in the Park. In all these important relations he has ever about the same time received a kind glance, or a blow of a fan, from some celebrated beauty, mother of the present Lord Such-a-one. This way of talking of his very much enlivens the conversation among us of a more sedate turn; and I find there is not one of the company, but myself, who rarely speak at all, but speaks of him as of that sort of man who is usually called a well-bred gentleman. To conclude his character, where women are not concerned, he is an honest, worthy man.

I cannot tell whether I am to account him whom I am next to speak of as one of our company, for he visits us but seldom; but when he does, it adds to every man else a new enjoyment of himself. He is a clergyman, a very philosophic man, of general learing, great sanctity of life, and the most exact good breeding. He has the misfortune to be of a very weak constitution, and, consequently, cannot accept of such cares and business as preferments in his function would oblige him to: he is, therefore, among divines what a chamber counsellor is among lawyers.

JOSEPH ADDISON

The probity of his mind and the integrity of his life create him followers, as being eloquent or loud advances others. He seldom introduces the subject he speaks upon; but we are so far gone in years, that he observes, when he is among us, an earnestness to have him fall on some divine topic, which he always treats with much authority, as one who has no interests in this world, as one who is hastening to the object of all his wishes, and conceives hope from his decays and infirmities. These are my ordinary companions.

JOSEPH ADDISON

Having often received an invitation from my friend Sir Roger de Coverley to pass away a month with him in the country, I last week accompanied him thither, and am settled with him for some time at his country house, where I intend to form several of my ensuing speculations. Sir Roger, who is very well acquainted with my humour, lets me rise and go to bed when I please, dine at his own table or in my chamber as I think fit, sit still and say nothing without bidding me be merry. When the gentlemen of the country come to see him, he only shews me at a distance: as I have been walking in his fields I have observed them stealing a sight of me over an hedge, and have heard the knight desiring them not to let me see them, for that I hated to be stared at.

I am the more at ease in Sir Roger's family, because it consists of sober and staid persons; for as the knight is the best master in the world, he seldom changes his servants; and as he is beloved by all about him, his servants never care for leaving him; by this means his domestics are all in years, and grown old with their master. You would take his valet-de-chambre for his brother, his butler is grey-headed, his groom is one of the gravest men that I have ever seen, and his coachman has the looks of a privy-counsellor. You see the goodness of the master even in the old house-dog, and in a grey pad that is kept in the stable with great care and tenderness out of regard to his past services, though he has been useless for several years.

I could not but observe with a great deal of pleasure the joy that appeared in the countenances of these ancient domestics upon my friend's arrival at his country-seat. Some of them could not refrain from tears at the sight of their old master; every one of them pressed forward to do something for him, and seemed discouraged if they were not employed. At the same time the good old knight, with a mixture of the father and the master of the family, tempered the enquiries after his own affairs with several kind questions relating to themselves. This humanity and good nature engages everybody to him, so that when he is pleasant upon any of them, all his family are in good humour, and none so much as the person whom he diverts himself with: on the contrary, if he coughs, or betrays any infirmity of old age, it is easy for a stander-by to observe a secret concern in the looks of all his servants.

My worthy friend has put me under the particular care of his butler, who is a very prudent man, and, as well as the rest of his fellow-servants, wonderfully desirous of pleasing me, because they have often heard their master talk of me as of his particular friend.

My chief companion, when Sir Roger is diverting himself in the woods or the fields, is a very venerable man who is ever with Sir Roger, and has lived at his house in the nature of a chaplain above thirty years. This gentleman is a person of good sense and some learning, of a very regular life and obliging conversation. He heartily loves Sir Roger, and knows that he is very much in the old Knight's esteem, so that he lives in the family rather as a relation than a dependant.

I have observed in several of my papers, that my friend Sir Roger, amidst all his good qualities, is something of an humorist; and that his virtues, as well as imperfections, are as it were tinged by a certain extravagance, which makes them particularly his, and distinguishes them from those of other men. This cast of mind, as it is generally very innocent in itself, so it renders his conversation highly agreeable, and more delightful than the same degree of sense and virtue would appear in their common and ordinary colours. As I was walking with him last night, he asked me how I liked the good man whom I have just now mentioned? and without staying for my answer told me, that he was afraid of being insulted with Latin and Greek at his own table; for which reason he desired a particular friend of his at the University to find him out a Clergyman rather of plain sense than much learning, of a good aspect, a clear voice, a sociable temper, and, if possible, a man that understood a little of backgammon. My friend, says Sir Roger, found me out this gentleman, who, besides the endowments required of him, is, they tell me, a good scholar, though he does not show it. I have given him the parsonage of the parish; and because I know his value have settled upon him a good annuity for life. If he outlives me, he shall find that he was higher in my esteem than perhaps he thinks he is. He has now been with me thirty years; and though he does not know I have taken notice of it, has never in all that time asked anything of me for himself, though he is

every day soliciting me for something in
behalf of one or other of my tenants his
parishioners. There has not been a lawsuit in the parish since he has lived among
them : If any dispute arises they apply themselves to him for the decision ; if they do
not acquiesce in his judgment, which I think
never happened above once or twice at most,
they appeal to me. At his first settling with me,
I made him a present of all the good sermons
which have been printed in English, and only
begged of him that every Sunday he would
pronounce one of them in the pulpit. Accordingly, he has digested them into such a
series, that they follow one another naturally,
and make a continued system of practical
divinity.

As Sir Roger was going on in his story,
the gentleman we were talking of came up
to us ; and upon the knight's asking him
who preached to-morrow (for it was Saturday
night) told us, the Bishop of St. Asaph in
the morning, and Dr. South in the afternoon.
He then showed us his list of preachers for
the whole year, where I saw with a great
deal of pleasure Archbishop Tillotson, Bishop
Saunderson, Doctor Barrow, Doctor Calamy,
with several living authors who have published
discourses of practical divinity. I no sooner
saw this venerable man in the pulpit, but I
very much approved of my friend's insisting
upon the qualifications of a good aspect and

a clear voice ; for I was so charmed with the gracefulness of his figure and delivery, as well as with the discourses he pronounced, that I think I never passed any time more to my satisfaction. A sermon repeated after this manner, is like the composition of a poet in the mouth of a graceful actor.

I could heartily wish that more of our country clergy would follow this example ; and instead of wasting their spirits in laborious compositions of their own, would endeavour after a handsome elocution, and all those other talents that are proper to enforce what has been penned by greater masters. This would not only be more easy to themselves, but more edifying to the people.

As I was yesterday morning walking with Sir Roger before his house, a country-fellow brought him a huge fish, which, he told him, Mr. William Wimble had caught that very morning ; and that he presented it, with his service to him, and intended to come and dine with him. At the same time he delivered a letter, which my friend read to me as soon as the messenger left him.

'Sir Roger,—I desire you to accept of a jack, which is the best I have caught this season. I intend to come and stay with you a week, and see how the perch bite in the

Black River. I observed with some concern,
the last time I saw you upon the bowling-
green, that your whip wanted a lash to it ;
I will bring half a dozen with me that I
twisted last week, which I hope will serve
you all the time you are in the country. I
have not been out of the saddle for six days
last past, having been at Eaton with Sir
John's eldest son. He takes to his learning
hugely.—I am, sir, your humble servant,
                                        Will Wimble.'

This extraordinary letter, and message that
accompanied it, made me very curious to
know the character and quality of the gentleman who sent them ; which I found to be as
follows. Will Wimble is younger brother
to a baronet, and descended of the ancient
family of the Wimbles. He is now between
forty and fifty ; but being bred to no business
and born to no estate, he generally lives with
his elder brother as superintendent of his
game. He hunts a pack of dogs better than
any man in the country, and is very famous
for finding out a hare. He is extremely well
versed in all the little handicrafts of an idle
man : He makes a may-fly to a miracle ; and
furnishes the whole country with angle-rods.
As he is a good-natured officious fellow, and
very much esteemed upon account of his
family, he is a welcome guest at every house,
and keeps up a good correspondence among

all the gentlemen about him. He carries a
tulip-root in his pocket from one to another,
or exchanges a puppy between a couple of
friends that live perhaps in the opposite sides
of the county. Will is a particular favourite
of all the young heirs, whom he frequently
cbliges with a net that he has weaved, or a
setting-dog that he has made himself: He
now and then presents a pair of garters of
his own knitting to their mothers or sisters;
and raises a great deal of mirth among them,
by inquiring as often as he meets them how
they wear? These gentleman-like manufactures and obliging little humours, make Will
the darling of the country.

Sir Roger was proceeding in the character
of him, when we saw him make up to us
with two or three hazel-twigs in his hand
that he had cut in Sir Roger's woods, as
he came through them, in his way to the
house. I was very much pleased to observe
on one side the hearty and sincere welcome
with which Sir Roger received him, and on
the other, the secret joy which his guest
discovered at sight of the good old knight.
After the first salutes were over, Will desired
Sir Roger to lend him one of his servants to
carry a set of shuttlecocks he had with him
in a little box to a lady that lived about a
mile off, to whom it seems he had promised
such a present for above this half year. Sir
Roger's back was no sooner turned but

honest Will began to tell me of a large cock-pheasant that he had sprung in one of the neighbouring woods, with two or three other adventures of the same nature. Odd and uncommon characters are the game that I look for, and most delight in ; for which reason I was as much pleased with the novelty of the person that talked to me, as he could be for his life with the springing of a pheasant, and therefore listened to him with more than ordinary attention.

In the midst of his discourse the bell rung to dinner, where the gentleman I have been speaking of had the pleasure of seeing the huge jack, he had caught, served up for the first dish in a most sumptuous manner. Upon our sitting down to it, he gave us a long account how he had hooked it, played with it, foiled it, and at length drew it out upon the bank, with several other particulars that lasted all the first course. A dish of wild-fowl that came afterwards furnished conversation for the rest of the dinner, which concluded with a late invention of Will's for improving the quail-pipe.

Upon withdrawing into my room after dinner, I was secretly touched with compassion towards the honest gentleman that had dined with us; and could not but consider with a great deal of concern, how so good an heart and such busy hands were wholly employed in trifles; that so much humanity should be so little beneficial to others, and so much industry so little advantageous to himself. The same temper of mind and application to affairs might have recommended him to the public esteem, and have raised his fortune in another station of life. What good to his country or himself might not a trader or merchant have done with such useful though ordinary qualifications?

Will Wimble's is the case of many a younger brother of a great family, who had rather see their children starve like gentlemen, than thrive in a trade or profession that is beneath their quality. This humour fills several parts of Europe with pride and beggary. It is the happiness of a trading nation, like ours, that the younger sons, though uncapable of any liberal art or profession, may be placed in such a way of life, as may perhaps enable them to vie with the best of their family: Accordingly we find several citizens that were launched into the world with narrow fortunes, rising by an honest industry to greater estates than those of their elder brothers. It is not improbable but Will was formerly tried at Divinity, Law, or Physic; and that finding his genius did not lie that way, his parents gave him up at length to his own inventions. But certainly, however improper he might have been for studies of a higher nature, he was perfectly well turned for the occupations of trade and commerce. As I think this is a point which cannot be too much inculcated, I shall desire my reader to compare what I have here written with what I have said in my twenty-first speculation.

RICHARD STEELE

I was this morning walking in the gallery, when Sir Roger entered at the end opposite to me, and advancing towards me, said, he was glad to meet me among his relations the de Coverleys, and hoped I liked the conversation of so much good company, who were as silent as myself. I knew he alluded to the pictures, and as he is a gentle-man who does not a little value himself upon his ancient descent, I expected he would give me some account of them. We were now arrived at the upper end of the gallery, when the knight faced towards one of the pictures, and as we stood before it, he entered into the matter, after his blunt way of saying things, as they occur to his imagination, without regular introduction, or care to preserve the appearance of chain of thought.

'It is,' said he, 'worth while to consider the force of dress; and how the persons of one age differ from those of another, merely by

that only. One may observe also, that the
general fashion of one age has been followed
by one particular set of people in another,
and by them preserved from one generation
to another. Thus the vast jetting coat and
small bonnet, which was the habit in Harry
the Seventh's time, is kept on in the Yeoman
of the Guard ; not without a good and politic
view, because they look a foot taller, and a
foot and a half broader: Besides that the
cap leaves the face expanded, and consequently more terrible, and fitter to stand at
the entrance of palaces.

'This predecessor of ours, you see, is
dressed after this manner, and his cheeks
would be no larger than mine, were he in a
hat as I am. He was the last man that
won a prize in the Tilt-Yard (which is now
a common street before Whitehall). You
see the broken lance that lies there by his
right foot: He shivered that lance of his
adversary all to pieces ; and bearing himself,
look you, sir, in this manner, at the same
time he came within the target of the gentleman who rode against him, and taking him
with incredible force before him on the
pommel of his saddle, he in that manner rid
the tournament over, with an air that showed
he did it rather to perform the rule of the
lists, than expose his enemy ; however, it
appeared he knew how to make use of a
victory, and with a gentle trot he marched

133

up to a gallery where their mistress sat (for they were rivals) and let him down with laudable courtesy and pardonable insolence. I don't know but it might be exactly where the coffee-house is now.

'You are to know this my ancestor was not only of a military genius, but fit also for the arts of peace, for he played on the bass-viol as well as any gentleman at court; you see where his viol hangs by his basket-hilt sword. The action at the Tilt-yard you may be sure won the fair lady, who was a maid of honour, and the greatest beauty of her time; here she stands, the next picture. You see, sir, my great great great grand-mother has on the new-fashioned petticoat, except that the modern is gathered at the waist; my grandmother appears as if she stood in a large drum, whereas the ladies now walk as if they were in a go-cart. For all this lady was bred at court she became an excellent country-wife, she brought ten children, and when I show you the library, you shall see in her own hand (allowing for the difference of the language) the best receipt now in England both for an hasty-pudding and a white-pot.

'If you please to fall back a little, because it is necessary to look at the three next pictures at one view; these are three sisters. She on the right hand, who is so very beautiful, died a maid; the next to her, still

handsomer, had the same fate, against her
will; this homely thing in the middle had
both their portions added to her own, and
was stolen by a neighbouring gentleman, a
man of stratagem and resolution, for he
poisoned three mastiffs to come at her, and
knocked down two deer-stealers in carrying
her off. Misfortunes happen in all families:
The theft of this romp and so much money,
was no great matter to our estate. But the
next heir that possessed it was this soft
gentleman, whom you see there: Observe
the small buttons, the little boots, the laces,
the slashes about his clothes, and above all
the posture he is drawn in (which to be sure
was his own choosing); you see he sits with
one hand on a desk writing, and looking as
it were another way, like an easy writer, or
a sonneteer: He was one of those that had
too much wit to know how to live in the
world; he was a man of no justice, but great
good manners; he ruined everybody that
had anything to do with him, but never said
a rude thing in his life; the most indolent
person in the world, he would sign a deed
that passed away half his estate with his
gloves on, but would not put on his hat
before a lady if it were to save his country.
He is said to be the first that made love by
squeezing the hand. He left the estate with
ten thousand pounds debt upon it, but however by all hands I have been informed that

RICHARD STEELE

he was every way the finest gentleman in
the world. That debt lay heavy on our
house for one generation, but it was re-
trieved by a gift from that honest man you
see there, a citizen of our name, but nothing
at all akin to us. I know Sir Andrew
Freeport has said behind my back, that this
man was descended from one of the ten
children of the maid of honour I showed
you above ; but it was never made out. We
winked at the thing indeed, because money
was wanting at that time.'

Here I saw my friend a little embarrassed,
and turned my face to the next portraiture.

Sir Roger went on with his account of
the gallery in the following manner. 'This
man (pointing to him I looked at) I take to
be the honour of our house. Sir Humphrey
de Coverley; he was in his dealings as
punctual as a tradesman, and as generous
as a gentleman. He would have thought
himself as much undone by breaking his
word, as if it were to be followed by
bankruptcy. He served his country as knight
of this shire to his dying day. He found it
no easy matter to maintain an integrity in
his words and actions, even in things that
regarded the offices which were incumbent
upon him, in the care of his own affairs and
relations of life, and therefore dreaded (though
he had great talents) to go into employments
of State, where he must be exposed to the

snares of ambition. Innocence of life and
great ability were the distinguishing parts
of his character; the latter, he had often
observed, had led to the destruction of the
former, and used frequently to lament that
great and good had not the same signification. He was an excellent husbandman, but
had resolved not to exceed such a degree of
wealth; all above it he bestowed in secret
bounties many years after the sum he aimed
at for his own use was attained. Yet he
did not slacken his industry, but to a decent
old age spent the life and fortune which was
superfluous to himself, in the service of his
friends and neighbours.'

Here we were called to dinner, and Sir
Roger ended the discourse of this gentleman,
by telling me, as we followed the servant,
that this his ancestor was a brave man, and
narrowly escaped being killed in the Civil
Wars; 'For,' said he, 'he was sent out of
the field upon a private message, the day
before the battle of Worcester.' The whim
of narrowly escaping by having been within
a day of danger, with other matters above-
mentioned, mixed with good sense, left me
at a loss whether I was more delighted with
my friend's wisdom or simplicity.

JOSEPH ADDISON

('Spectator,' No. 110.)

At a little distance from Sir Roger's house, among the ruins of an old abbey, there is a long walk of aged elms; which are shot up so very high, that when one passes under them, the Rooks and Crows that rest upon the tops of them seem to be cawing in another region. I am very much delighted with this sort of noise, which I consider as a kind of natural prayer to that being who supplies the wants of his whole creation, and who, in the beautiful language of the Psalms, feedeth the young ravens that call upon him. I like this retirement the better, because of an ill report it lies under of being haunted; for which reason (as I have been told in the family) no living creature ever walks in it besides the chaplain. My good friend the butler desired me with a very grave face not to venture myself in it after sunset, for that one of the footmen had been almost frightened out of his wits by a spirit that appeared to him in the shape of a black horse without an head; to which he added, that about a month ago one of the maids coming home late that way with a pail of milk upon her head, heard such a rustling among the bushes that she let it fall.

JOSEPH ADDISON

I was taking a walk in this place last
night between the hours of nine and ten,
and could not but fancy it one of the most
proper scenes in the world for a ghost to
appear in. The ruins of the abbey are
scattered up and down on every side, and
half-covered with ivy and elder-bushes, the
harbours of several solitary birds which
seldom make their appearance till the dusk
of the evening. The place was formerly a
church-yard, and has still several marks in
it of graves and burying-places. There is
such an echo among the old ruins and vaults,
that if you stamp but a little louder than
ordinary, you hear the sound repeated. At
the same time the walk of elms, with the
croaking of the ravens which from time to
time are heard from the tops of them, looks
exceeding solemn and venerable. These
objects naturally raise seriousness and attention; and when night heightens the aw-
fulness of the place, and pours out her
supernumerary horrors upon everything in
it, I do not at all wonder that weak minds
fill it with spectres and apparitions.

Mr. Locke, in his chapter on the associa-
tion of ideas, has very curious remarks to
show how by the prejudice of education one
idea often introduces into the mind a whole
set that bear no resemblance to one another
in the nature of things. Among several
examples of this kind, he produces the

following instance. 'The ideas of goblins
and sprites have really no more to do with
darkness than light: Yet let but a foolish
maid inculcate these often on the mind of a
child, and raise them there together, possibly
he shall never be able to separate them again
so long as he lives: but darkness shall ever
afterwards bring with it those frightful ideas,
and they shall be so joined, that he can no
more bear the one than the other.'

As I was walking in this solitude, where
the dusk of the evening conspired with so
many other occasions of terror, I observed
a cow grazing not far from me, which an
imagination that is apt to startle might
easily have construed into a black horse
without an head: And I dare say the poor
footman lost nis wits upon some such trivial
occasion.

My friend Sir Roger has often told me
with a great deal of mirth, that at his first
coming to his estate he found three parts of
his house altogether useless; that the best
room in it had the reputation of being
haunted, and by that means was locked up;
that noises had been heard in his long
gallery, so that he could not get a servant
to enter it after eight o'clock at night; that
the door of one of his chambers was nailed
up, because there went a story in the family
that a butler had formerly hanged himself in
it; and that his mother, who lived to a great

age, had shut up half the rooms in the house, in which either her husband, a son, or daughter had died. The Knight seeing his habitation reduced to so small a compass, and himself in a manner shut out of his own house, upon the death of his mother ordered all the apartments to be flung open, and exorcised by his Chaplain, who lay in every room one after another, and by that means dissipated the fears which had so long reigned in the family.

I should not have been thus particular upon these ridiculous horrors, did I not find them so very much prevail in all parts of the country. At the same time I think a person who is thus terrified with the imagination of ghosts and spectres much more reasonable than one who, contrary to the reports of all historians sacred and profane, ancient and modern, and to the traditions of all nations, thinks the appearance of spirits fabulous and groundless: Could not I give myself up to this general testimony of mankind, I should to the relations of particular persons who are now living, and whom I cannot distrust in other matters of fact. I might here add, that not only the historians, to whom we may join the poets, but likewise the philosophers of antiquity have favoured this opinion. Lucretius himself, though by the course of his philosophy he was obliged to maintain that the soul did not exist separate

from the body, makes no doubt of the
reality of apparitions, and that men have
often appeared after their death. This I
think very remarkable; he was so pressed
with the matter of fact which he could not
have the confidence to deny, that he was
forced to account for it by one of the most
absurd unphilosophical notions that was ever
started. He tells us, that the surface of all
bodies are perpetually flying off from their
respective bodies, one after another; and
that these surfaces or thin cases that included each other whilst they were joined
in the body like the coats of an onion, are
sometimes seen entire when they are separated from it; by which means we often
behold the shapes and shadows of persons
who are either dead or absent.

I shall dismiss this paper with a story out
of Josephus, not so much for the sake of the
story itself as for the moral reflections with
which the author concludes it, and which
I shall here set down in his own words.
'Glaphyra the daughter of King Archelaus,
after the death of her two first husbands
(being married to a third, who was brother
to her first husband, and so passionately in
love with her that he turned off his former
wife to make room for this marriage) had a
very odd kind of dream. She fancied that
she saw her first husband coming towards
her, and that she embraced him with great

tenderness; when in the midst of the pleasure
which she expressed at the sight of him,
he reproached her after the following manner:
Glaphyra, says he, thou hast made good the
old saying, that women are not to be trusted.
Was not I the husband of thy virginity?
Have I not children by thee? How couldst
thou forget our loves so far as to enter into
a second marriage, and after that into a
third, nay to take for thy husband a man
who has so shamelessly crept into the bed of
his brother? However, for the sake of our
past loves, I shall free thee from thy present
reproach, and make thee mine for ever.
Glaphyra told this dream to several women
of her acquaintance, and died soon after. I
thought this story might not be impertinent
in this place, wherein I speak of those kings:
Besides that, the example deserves to be
taken notice of as it contains a most certain
proof of the immortality of the soul, and of
divine providence. If any man thinks these
facts incredible, let him enjoy his own opinion
to himself, but let him not endeavour to
disturb the belief of others, who by instances
of this nature are excited to the study of
virtue.'

('Spectator,' No. 117.)

There are some opinions in which a man
should stand neuter, without engaging his
assent to one side or the other. Such a

143

hovering faith as this, which refuses to settle
upon any determination, is absolutely necessary to a mind that is careful to avoid errors
and prepossessions. When the arguments
press equally on both sides in matters that are
indifferent to us, the safest method is to give
up our selves to neither.

It is with this temper of mind that I consider the subject of witchcraft. When I hear
the relations that are made from all parts of
the world, not only from Norway and Lap-
land, from the East and West Indies, but
from every particular nation in Europe, I cannot forbear thinking that there is such an
intercourse and commerce with evil spirits, as
that which we express by the name of Witchcraft. But when I consider that the ignorant
and credulous parts of the world abound most
in these relations, and that the persons among
us, who are supposed to engage in such an
infernal commerce, are people of a weak
understanding and a crazed imagination, and
at the same time reflect upon the many im-
postures and delusions of this nature that
have been detected in all ages, I endeavour
to suspend my belief till I hear more certain
accounts than any which have yet come to
my knowledge. In short, when I consider
the question, whether there are such persons
in the world as those we call witches? my
mind is divided between the two opposite
opinions; or rather (to speak my thoughts

freely) I believe in general that there is, and has been such a thing as witchcraft; but at the same time can give no credit to any particular instance of it.

I am engaged in this speculation, by some occurrences that I met with yesterday, which I shall give my reader an account of at large. As I was walking with my friend Sir Roger by the side of one of his woods, an old woman applied herself to me for my charity. Her dress and figure put me in mind of the following description in ' Otway ' :

> In a close lane as I pursu'd my journey,
> I spy'd a wrinkled hag, with age grown double,
> Picking dry sticks, and mumbling to herself.
> Her eyes with scalding rheum were gall'd and red,
> Cold palsy shook her head; her hands seem'd wither'd;
> And on her crooked shoulders had she wrap'd
> The tatter'd remnants of an old striped hanging,
> Which served to keep her carcase from the cold :
> So there was nothing of a piece about her.
> Her lower weeds were all o'er coarsely patch'd
> With diff'rent colour'd rags, black, red, white, yellow,
> And seem'd to speak variety of wretchedness.

As I was musing on this description, and comparing it with the object before me, the Knight told me that this very old woman had

the reputation of a witch all over the country,
that her lips were observed to be always in
motion, and that there was not a switch
about her house which her neighbours did
not believe had carried her several hundreds
of miles. If she chanced to stumble, they
always found sticks or straws that lay in the
figure of a cross before her. If she made any
mistake at church, and cried 'Amen' in the
wrong place, they never failed to conclude
that she was saying her prayers backwards.
There was not a maid in the parish that would
take a pin of her, though she would offer a
bag of money with it. She goes by the name
of Moll White, and has made the country ring
with several imaginary exploits which are
palmed upon her. If the dairy maid does not
make her butter come so soon as she should
have it, Moll White is at the bottom of the
churn. If a horse sweats in the stable, Moll
White has been upon his back. If a hare
makes an unexpected escape from the hounds,
the huntsman curses Moll White. Nay (says
Sir Roger), I have known the Master of the
Pack, upon such an occasion, send one of his
servants to see if Moll White had been out
that morning.

This account raised my curiosity so far,
that I begged my friend Sir Roger to go with
me into her hovel, which stood in a solitary
corner under the side of the wood. Upon
our first entering Sir Roger winked to me,

and pointed at something that stood behind the door, which, upon looking that way, I found to be an old broomstaff. At the same time he whispered me in the ear to take notice of a tabby cat that sat in the chimney-corner, which, as the old Knight told me, lay under as bad a report as Moll White herself; for besides that Moll is said often to accompany her in the same shape, the cat is reported to have spoken twice or thrice in her life, and to have played several pranks above the capacity of an ordinary cat.

I was secretly concerned to see human nature in so much wretchedness and disgrace, but at the same time could not forbear smiling to hear Sir Roger, who is a little puzzled about the old woman, advising her as a Justice of Peace to avoid all communication with the devil; and never to hurt any of her neighbours' cattle. We concluded our visit with a bounty, which was very acceptable.

In our return home, Sir Roger told me that old Moll had been often brought before him for making children spit pins, and giving maids the nightmare; and that the country people would be tossing her into a pond and trying experiments with her every day, if it was not for him and his chaplain.

I have since found upon enquiry, that Sir Roger was several times staggered with the reports that had been brought him concerning this old woman, and would frequently have bound her over to the County Sessions, had not his chaplain with much ado persuaded him to the contrary.

I have been the more particular in this account, because I hear there is scarce a village in England that has not a Moll White in it. When an old woman begins to doat, and grow chargeable to a parish, she is generally turned into a witch, and fills the whole country with extravagant fancies, imaginary distempers, and terrifying dreams. In the mean time, the poor wretch that is the innocent occasion of so many evils begins to be frightened at her self, and sometimes confesses secret commerce and familiarities that her imagination forms in a delirious old age. This frequently cuts off charity from the greatest objects of compassion, and inspires people with a malevolence towards those poor decrepit parts of our species, in whom human nature is defaced by infirmity and dotage.

'Spectator,' No. 112.)

I am always very well pleased with a country Sunday; and think, if keeping holy the seventh day were only a human institution, it would be the best method that could have been thought of for the polishing and civilising of mankind. It is certain the country-people would soon degenerate into a kind of savages and barbarians, were there not such frequent returns of a stated time, in which the whole village meet together with their best faces, and in their cleanliest habits, to converse with one another upon indifferent subjects, hear their duties explained to them, and join together in adoration of the Supreme Being. Sunday clears away the rust of the whole week, not only as it refreshes in their minds the notions of religion, but as it puts both the sexes upon appearing in their most agreeable forms, and exerting all such qualities as are apt to give them a figure in the eye of the village. A country-fellow distinguishes himself as much in the church-yard, as a citizen does upon the 'change, the whole parish-politics being generally discussed in that place either after sermon or before the bell rings.

My friend Sir Roger, being a good Churchman, has beautified the inside of his church with several texts of his own choosing: he has likewise given a handsome pulpit-cloth, and railed in the communion-table at his own expense. He has often told me, that at his coming to his estate he found his parishioners very irregular; and that in order to make them kneel and join in the responses, he gave every one of them a hassock and a Common-prayer Book: and at the same time employed an itinerant singing-master, who goes about the country for that purpose, to instruct them rightly in the tunes of the Psalms; upon which they now very much value themselves, and indeed out-do most of the country churches that I have ever heard.

As Sir Roger is landlord to the whole congregation, he keeps them in very good order, and will suffer nobody to sleep in it besides himself; for if by chance he has been surprised into a short nap at sermon, upon recovering out of it he stands up and looks about him, and if he sees anybody else nodding, either wakes them himself, or sends his servant to them. Several other of the old Knight's particularities break out upon these occasions : sometimes he will be lengthening out a verse in the singing-Psalms, half a minute after the rest of the congregation have done with it ; sometimes, when he is pleased with the matter of his devotion, he pronounces 'Amen' three or four times to the same prayer ; and sometimes stands up when everybody else is upon their knees, to count the congregation, or see if any of his tenants are missing.

I was yesterday very much surprised to hear my old friend, in the midst of the service, calling out to one John Matthews to mind what he was about, and not disturb the congregation. This John Matthews it seems is remarkable for being an idle fellow, and at the time was kicking his heels for his diversion. This authority of the Knight, though exerted in that odd manner which accompanies him in all circumstances of life, has a very good effect upon the parish, who are not polite enough to see any thing ridiculous in his behaviour; besides that the general good sense and worthiness of his character makes his friends observe these little singularities as foils that rather set off than blemish his good qualities.

As soon as the sermon is finished, nobody presumes to stir till Sir Roger is gone out of the church. The Knight walks down from his seat in the chancel between a double row of his tenants, that stand bowing to him on each side; and every now and then enquires how such an one's wife, or mother, or son, or father do, whom he does not see at church; which is understood as a secret reprimand to the person that is absent.

The chaplain has often told me, that upon a catechising-day, when Sir Roger has been pleased with a boy that answers well, he has ordered a Bible to be given him next day for his encouragement; and sometimes accompanies it with a flitch of bacon to his mother. Sir Roger has likewise added five pounds a year to the clerk's place; and that he may encourage the young fellows to make themselves perfect in the Church service, has promised upon the death of the present incumbent, who is very old, to bestow it according to merit.

The fair understanding between Sir Roger

and his chaplain, and their mutual concurrence in doing good, is the more remarkable,
because the very next village is famous for
the differences and contentions that rise
between the Parson and the Squire, who
live in a perpetual state of war. The Parson
is alway preaching at the Squire, and the
Squire to be revenged on the Parson never
comes to church. The Squire has made all
his tenants Atheists and tithe-stealers; while
the Parson instructs them every Sunday in
the dignity of his order, and insinuates to
them in almost every sermon, that he is a
better man than his patron. In short, matters
are come to such an extremity, that the Squire
has not said his prayers either in public or
private this half year; and that the Parson
threatens him, if he does not mend his
manners, to pray for him in the face of the
whole congregation.

Feuds of this nature, though too frequent
in the country, are very fatal to the ordinary
people; who are so used to be dazzled with
riches, that they pay as much deference to the
understanding of a man of an estate, as of a
man of learning; and are very hardly brought
to regard any truth, how important soever it
may be, that is preached to them, when they
know there are several men of five hundred a
year who do not believe it.

('Spectator,' No. 122.)

A man's first care should be to avoid the
reproaches of his own heart; his next, to
escape the censures of the world: if the last
interferes with the former, it ought to be
entirely neglected; but otherwise, there cannot be a greater satisfaction to an honest
mind, than to see those approbations which
it gives itself seconded by the applauses of
the public: a man is more sure of his conduct,
when the verdict which he passes upon his
own behaviour is thus warranted and confirmed by the opinion of all that know him.

My worthy friend Sir Roger is one of those
who is not only at peace within himself, but
beloved and esteemed by all about him. He
receives a suitable tribute for his universal
benevolence to mankind, in the returns of
affection and good-will, which are paid him
by every one that lives within his neighbourhood. I lately met with two or three odd
instances of that general respect which is
shown to the good old knight. He would
needs carry Will Wimble and myself with
him to the County Assizes. As we were upon
the road, Will Wimble joined a couple of
plain men who rid before us, and conversed
with them for some time; during which my
friend Sir Roger acquainted me with their
characters.

The first of them, says he, that has a spaniel

by his side, is a yeoman of about an hundred
pounds a year, an honest man: he is just
within the Game Act, and qualified to kill
an hare or a pheasant: he knocks down a
dinner with his gun twice or thrice a week;
and by that means lives much cheaper than
those who have not so good an estate as himself. He would be a good neighbour if he
did not destroy so many partridges; in short,
he is a very sensible man; shoots flying; and
has been several times foreman of the Petty
Jury.

The other that rides along with him is Tom
Touchy, a fellow famous for 'taking the law'
of everybody. There is not one in the town
where he lives that he has not sued at the
Quarter Sessions. The rogue had once the
impudence to go to law with the Widow.
His head is full of costs, damages, and eject-
ments: he plagued a couple of honest gentlemen so long for a trespass in breaking one
of his hedges, till he was forced to sell the
ground it enclosed to defray the charges of
the prosecution. His father left him fourscore
pounds a year; but he has cast and been cast
so often, that he is not now worth thirty. I
suppose he is going upon the old business of
the willow-tree.

As Sir Roger was giving me this account
of Tom Touchy, Will Wimble and his two
companions stopped short till we came up to
them. After having paid their respects to

Sir Roger, Will told him that Mr. Touchy
and he must appeal to him upon a dispute
that arose between them. Will, it seems,
had been giving his fellow-traveller an
account of his angling one day in such a
hole ; when Tom Touchy, instead of hearing
out his story, told him that Mr. Such-an-One,
if he pleased, might take the law of him for
fishing in that part of the river. My friend
Sir Roger heard them both, upon a round
trot ; and after having paused some time, told
them, with the air of a man who would not
give his judgment rashly, that much might
be said on both sides. They were neither of
them dissatisfied with the Knight's determination, because neither of them found himself in
the wrong by it: upon which we made the
best of our way to the assizes.

The court was sat before Sir Roger came ;
but notwithstanding all the justices had taken
their places upon the bench, they made room
for the old Knight at the head of them ; who
for his reputation in the country took occasion
to whisper in the judge's ear, That he was
glad his lordship had met with so much good
weather in his circuit. I was listening to the
proceeding of the court with much attention,
and infinitely pleased with that great appearance and solemnity which so properly accompanies such a public administration of our
laws ; when, after about an hour's sitting, I
observed, to my great surprise, in the midst

of a trial, that my friend Sir Roger was getting up to speak. I was in some pain for him, till I found he had acquitted himself of two or three sentences, with a look of much business and great intrepidity.

Upon his first rising the court was hushed, and a general whisper ran among the country people that Sir Roger was up. The speech he made was so little to the purpose, that I shall not trouble my readers with an account of it; and I believe was not so much designed by the Knight himself to inform the court, as to give him a figure in my eye, and keep up his credit in the country.

I was highly delighted, when the court rose, to see the gentlemen of the country gathering about my old friend, and striving who should compliment him most; at the same time that the ordinary people gazed upon him at a distance, not a little admiring his courage, that was not afraid to speak to the judge.

In our return home we met with a very odd accident; which I cannot forbear relating, because it shows how desirous all who know Sir Roger are of giving him marks of their esteem. When we were arrived upon the verge of his estate, we stopped at a little inn to rest ourselves and our horses. The man of the house had, it seems, been formerly a servant in the Knight's family; and to do honour to his old master, had some time

since, unknown to Sir Roger, put him up
in a sign-post before the door; so that the
Knight's Head had hung out upon the road
about a week before he himself knew anything of the matter. As soon as Sir Roger
was acquainted with it, finding that his
servant's indiscretion proceeded wholly from
affection and good-will, he only told him that
he had made him too high a compliment;
and when the fellow seemed to think that
could hardly be, added with a more decisive
look, That it was far too great an honour for
any man under a duke; but told him at the
same time, that it might be altered with a
very few touches, and that he himself would
be at the charge of it. Accordingly they got
a painter by the Knight's directions to add a
pair of whiskers to the face, and by a little
aggravation to the features to change it into
the Saracen's Head. I should not have
known this story had not the inn-keeper,
upon Sir Roger's alighting, told him in my
hearing, That his honour's head was brought
back last night with the alterations that he
had ordered to be made in it. Upon this my
friend with his usual cheerfulness related the
particulars above-mentioned, and ordered the
head to be brought into the room. I could
not forbear discovering greater expressions
of mirth than ordinary upon the appearance
of this monstrous face, under which, notwithstanding it was made to frown and stare in

a most extraordinary manner, I could still
discover a distant resemblance of my old
friend. Sir Roger, upon seeing me laugh,
desired me to tell him truly if I thought it
possible for people to know him in that disguise. I at first kept my usual silence ; but
upon the Knight's conjuring me to tell him
whether it was not still more like himself
than a Saracen, I composed my countenance
in the best manner I could, and replied, That
much might be said on both sides.

These several adventures, with the Knight's
behaviour in them, gave me as pleasant a
day as ever I met with in any of my travels.

('Spectator,' No. 130.)

As I was yesterday riding out in the fields
with my friend Sir Roger, we saw at a little
distance from us a troop of gipsies. Upon
the first discovery of them, my friend was in
some doubt whether he should not exert the
justice of the peace upon such a band of lawless vagrants ; but not having his clerk with
him, who is a necessary counsellor on these
occasions, and fearing that his poultry might
fare the worse for it, he let the thought drop :
But at the same time gave me a particular
account of the mischiefs they do in the
country, in stealing people's goods and spoil-
ing their servants. If a stray piece of linen
hangs upon an hedge, says Sir Roger, they

are sure to have it ; if the hog loses his way
in the fields, it is ten to one but he becomes
their prey ; our geese cannot live in peace for
them ; if a man prosecutes them with severity,
his hen-roost is sure to pay for it : They
generally straggle into these parts about this
time of the year ; and set the heads of our
servant-maids so agog for husbands, that we
do not expect to have any business done as
it should be whilst they are in the country.
I have an honest dairy-maid who crosses their
hands with a piece of silver every summer,
and never fails being promised the hand-
somest young fellow in the parish for her
pains. Your friend the butler has been fool
enough to be seduced by them ; and, though
he is sure to lose a knife, a fork, or a spoon
every time his fortune is told him, generally
shuts himself up in the pantry with an old
gipsy for above half an hour once in a twelvemonth. Sweet-hearts are the things they
live upon, which they bestow very plentifully
upon all those that apply themselves to them.
You see now and then some handsome young
jades among them : The sluts have very often
white teeth and black eyes.

Sir Roger observing that I listened with
great attention to his account of a people who
were so entirely new to me, told me, that if I
would they should tell us our fortunes. As
I was very well pleased with the Knight's
proposal, we rid up and communicated our

hands to them. A Cassandra of the crew,
after having examined my lines very diligently, told me, That I loved a pretty maid
in a corner, that I was a good woman's
man, with some other particulars which I do
not think proper to relate. My friend Sir
Roger alighted from his horse, and exposing
his palm to two or three that stood by
him, they crumpled it into all shapes, and
diligently scanned every wrinkle that could
be made in it ; when one of them, who was
older and more sunburnt than the rest, told
him, That he had a widow in his line of life:
Upon which the Knight cried, Go, go, you
are an idle baggage ; and at the same time
smiled upon me. The gipsy finding he was
not displeased in his heart, told him, after a
farther enquiry into his hand, that his true-
love was constant, and that she should dream
of him to-night: My old friend cried Pish,
and bid her go on. The gipsy told him that
he was a bachelor, but would not be so
long ; and that he was dearer to somebody
than he thought : The Knight still repeated,
She was an idle baggage, and bid her go on.
Ah, master, says the gipsy, that roguish leer
of yours makes a pretty woman's heart ache ;
you ha'nt that simper about the mouth for
nothing. The uncouth gibberish with which
all this was uttered like the darkness of an
oracle, made us the more attentive to it. To
be short, the Knight left the money with her

that he had crossed her hand with, and got up again on his horse.

As we were riding away, Sir Roger told me, that he knew several sensible people who believed those gipsies now and then foretold very strange things ; and for half an hour together appeared more jocund than ordinary. In the height of his good-humour, meeting a common beggar upon the road who was no conjurer, as he went to relieve him he found his pocket was picked : that being a kind of palmistry at which this race of vermin are very dexterous.

I might here entertain my reader with historical remarks on this idle profligate people, who infest all the countries of Europe, and live in the midst of governments in a kind of commonwealth by themselves. But instead of entering into observations of this nature, I shall fill the remaining part of my paper with a story which is still fresh in Holland, and was printed in one of our monthly accounts about twenty years ago. 'As the Trekschuyt, or hackney-boat, which carries passengers from Leyden to Amsterdam, was putting off, a boy running along the side of the canal desired to be taken in ; which the master of the boat refused, because the lad had not quite money enough to pay the usual fare. An eminent merchant being pleased with the looks of the boy, and secretly touched with compassion towards him, paid the money for him, and ordered

L 161

him to be taken on board. Upon talking with
him afterwards, he found that he could speak
readily in three or four languages, and learned
upon farther examination that he had been
stolen away when he was a child by a gipsy,
and had rambled ever since with a gang of
those strollers up and down several parts of
Europe. It happened that the merchant,
whose heart seems to have inclined towards
the boy by a secret kind of instinct, had himself lost a child some years before. The
parents, after a long search for him, gave
him for drowned in one of the canals with
which that country abounds ; and the mother
was so afflicted at the loss of a fine boy, who
was her only son, that she died for grief of it.
Upon laying together all particulars, and
examining the several moles and marks by
which the mother used to describe the child
when he was first missing, the boy proved to
be the son of the merchant whose heart had
so unaccountably melted at the sight of him.
The lad was very well pleased to find a father
who was so rich, and likely to leave him a
good estate ; the father on the other hand
was not a little delighted to see a son return
to him, whom he had given for lost, with
such a strength of constitution, sharpness of
understanding, and skill in languages.' Here
the printed story leaves off ; but if I may give
credit to reports, our linguist having received
such extraordinary rudiments towards a good

education, was afterwards trained up in everything that becomes a gentleman ; wearing off
by little and little all the vicious habits and
practices that he had been used to in the
course of his peregrinations. Nay, it is said,
that he has since been employed in foreign
courts upon National business, with great
reputation to himself and honour to those who
sent him, and that he has visited several
countries as a public minister, in which he
formerly wandered as a gipsy.

RICHARD STEELE

('Spectator,' No. 174.)

There is scarce anything more common
than animosities between parties that cannot
subsist but by their agreement : this was well
represented in the sedition of the members of
the humane body in the old Roman fable. It
is often the case of lesser confederate states
against a superior Power, which are hardly
held together, though their unanimity is necessary for their common safety : and this is
always the case of the landed and trading
interest of Great Britain : the trader is fed by
the product of the land, and the landed man
cannot be clothed but by the skill of the
trader ; and yet those interests are ever
jarring.

We had last winter an instance of this at

our club, in Sir Roger de Coverley and Sir
Andrew Freeport, between whom there is
generally a constant, though friendly, opposition of opinions. It happened that one of the
company, in an historical discourse, was
observing, that Carthaginian faith was a pro-
verbial phrase to intimate breach of Leagues.
Sir Roger said it could hardly be otherwise:
That the Carthaginians were the greatest
traders in the world; and as gain is the chief
end of such a people, they never pursue any
other. The means to it are never regarded;
they will, if it comes easily, get money
honestly; but if not, they will not scruple to
attain it by fraud or cozenage: and indeed,
what is the whole business of the trader's
account, but to over-reach him who trusts to
his memory? But were that not so, what
can there great and noble be expected from
him whose attention is for ever fixed upon
balancing his books, and watching over his
expenses? And at best, let frugality and
parsimony be the virtues of the merchant,
how much is his punctual dealing below a
gentleman's charity to the poor, or hospitality
among his neighbours?

Captain Sentry observed Sir Andrew very
diligent in hearing Sir Roger, and had a
mind to turn the discourse, by taking notice
in general, from the highest to the lowest
parts of human society, there was a secret,
tho' unjust, way among men, of indulging

164

the seeds of ill-nature and envy, by comparing
their own state of life to that of another, and
grudging the approach of their neighbour to
their own happiness; and on the other side,
he who is the less at his ease, repines at the
other who, he thinks, has unjustly the advantage over him. Thus the civil and military
lists look upon each other with much ill-
nature; the soldier repines at the courtier's
power, and the courtier rallies the soldier's
honour; or, to come to lower instances, the
private men in the horse and foot of an army,
the carmen and coachmen in the city streets,
mutually look upon each other with ill-will,
when they are in competition for quarters or
the way, in their respective motions.

It is very well, good captain, interrupted
Sir Andrew, you may attempt to turn the
discourse if you think fit; but I must, however, have a word or two with Sir Roger,
who, I see, thinks he has paid me off, and
been very severe upon the merchant. I shall
not, continued he, at this time remind Sir
Roger of the great and noble monuments of
charity and public spirit which have been
erected by merchants since the Reformation,
but at present content myself with what he
allows us, parsimony and frugality. If it
were consistent with the quality of so ancient
a baronet as Sir Roger, to keep an account,
or measure things by the most infallible way,
that of numbers, he would prefer our parsi-

mony to his hospitality. If to drink so many hogsheads is to be hospitable, we do not contend for the fame of that virtue; but it would be worth while to consider, whether so many artificers at work ten days together by my appointment, or so many peasants made merry on Sir Roger's charge, are the men more obliged? I believe the families of the artificers will thank me, more than the households of the peasants shall Sir Roger. Sir Roger gives to his men, but I place mine above the necessity or obligation of my bounty. I am in very little pain for the Roman proverb upon the Carthaginian traders; the Romans were their professed enemies: I am only sorry no Carthaginian histories have come to our hands; we might have been taught, perhaps, by them some proverbs against the Roman generosity, in fighting for and bestowing other people's goods. But since Sir Roger has taken occasion from an old proverb to be out of humour with merchants, it should be no offence to offer one not quite so old in their defence. When a man happens to break in Holland, they say of him that 'he has not kept true accounts.' This phrase, perhaps, among us, would appear a soft or humorous way of speaking, but with that exact nation it bears the highest reproach; for a man to be mistaken in the calculation of his expense, in his ability to answer future demands, or to be impertinently sanguine in

putting his credit to too great adventure, are
all instances of as much infamy as with gayer
nations to be failing in courage or common
honesty.

Numbers are so much the measure of everything that is valuable, that it is not possible
to demonstrate the success of any action, or
the prudence of any undertaking, without
them. I say this in answer to what Sir Roger
is pleased to say, that little that is truly noble
can be expected from one who is ever poring
on his cash-book, or balancing his accounts.
When I have my returns from abroad, I can
tell to a shilling, by the help of numbers, the
profit or loss by my adventure; but I ought
also to be able to show that I had reason or
making it, either from my own experience
or that of other people, or from a reasonable
presumption that my returns will be sufficient
to answer my expense and hazard; and this
is never to be done without the skill of numbers. For instance, if I am to trade to Turkey,
I ought beforehand to know the demand of
our manufactures there, as well as of their
silks in England, and the customary prices
that are given for both in each country. I
ought to have a clear knowledge of these
matters beforehand, that I may presume upon
sufficient returns to answer the charge of the
cargo I have fitted out, the freight and assurance out and home, the custom to the queen,
and the interest of my own money, and besides

all these expenses a reasonable profit to myself. Now, what is there of scandal in this
skill? What has the merchant done, that
he should be so little in the good graces of
Sir Roger? He throws down no man's
enclosures, and tramples upon no man's
corn; he takes nothing from the industrious
labourer; he pays the poor man for his work;
he communicates his profit with mankind;
by the preparation of his cargo and the manu-
facture of his returns, he furnishes employment and subsistence to greater numbers
than the richest nobleman; and even the
nobleman is obliged to him for finding out
foreign markets for the produce of his estate,
and for making a great addition to his rents;
and yet 'tis certain, that none of all these
things could be done by him without the
exercise of his skill in numbers.

This is the economy of the merchant; and
the conduct of the gentleman must be the
same, unless by scorning to be the steward, he
resolves the steward shall be the gentleman.
The gentleman, no more than the merchant,
is able without the help of numbers to account
for the success of any action, or the prudence
of any adventure. If, for instance, the chase
is his whole adventure, his only returns must
be the stag's horns in the great hall, and the
fox's nose upon the stable-door. Without
doubt Sir Roger knows the full value of these
returns; and if beforehand he had computed

the charges of the chase, a gentleman of his
discretion would certainly have hanged up
all his dogs, he would never have brought
back so many fine horses to the kennel, he
would never have gone so often, like a blast,
over fields of corn. If such too had been the
conduct of all his ancestors, he might truly
have boasted at this day that the antiquity of
his family had never been sullied by a trade ;
a merchant had never been permitted with
his whole estate to purchase a room for his
picture in the gallery of the Coverleys, or to
claim his descent from the maid of honour.
But 'tis very happy for Sir Roger that the
merchant paid so dear for his ambition. 'Tis
the misfortune of many other gentlemen to
turn out of the seats of their ancestors, to
make way for such new masters as have been
more exact in their accounts than themselves ;
and certainly he deserves the estate a great
deal better who has got it by his industry,
than he who has lost it by his negligence.

JOSEPH ADDISON

('Spectator,' No. 269.)

I was this morning surprised with a great
knocking at the door, when my landlady's
daughter came up to me, and told me that
there was a man below desired to speak with
me. Upon my asking her who it was, she

told me it was a very grave elderly person, but that she did not know his name. I immediately went down to him, and found him to be the coachman of my worthy friend, Sir Roger de Coverley. He told me that his master came to town last night, and would be glad to take a turn with me in Gray's-Inn Walks. As I was wondering in myself what had brought Sir Roger to town, not having lately received any letter from him, he told me that his master was come up to get a sight of Prince Eugene, and that he desired I would immediately meet him.

I was not a little pleased with the curiosity of the old knight, though I did not much wonder at it, having heard him say more than once in private discourse that he looked upon Prince Eugenio (for so the Knight always calls him) to be a greater man than Scanderbeg.

I was no sooner come into Gray's-Inn Walks, but I heard my friend upon the terrace hemming twice or thrice to himself with great vigour, for he loves to clear his pipes in good air (to make use of his own phrase) and is not a little pleased with any one who takes notice of the strength which he still exerts in his morning hems.

I was touched with a secret joy at the sight of the good old man, who before he saw me was engaged in conversation with a beggar-man that had asked an alms of him. I could hear my friend chide him for not finding out some work; but at the same time saw him put his hand in his pocket and give him sixpence.

Our salutations were very hearty on both sides, consisting of many kind shakes of the hand, and several affectionate looks which we cast upon one another. After which the Knight told me my good friend his chaplain was very well, and much at my service, and that the Sunday before he had made a most incomparable sermon out of Dr. Barrow. I have left, says he, all my affairs in his hands, and being willing to lay an obligation upon him, have deposited with him thirty marks, to be distributed among his poor parishioners.

He then proceeded to acquaint me with the welfare of Will Wimble. Upon which he put his hand into his fob and presented me in his name with a tobacco-stopper, telling me that Will had been busy all the beginning of the winter in turning great quantities of them; and that he made a present of one to every gentleman in the country who has good principles and smokes. He added, that poor Will was at present under great tribulation, for that Tom Touchy had taken the law of him for cutting some hazel sticks out of one of his hedges.

Among other pieces of news which the Knight brought from his country-seat, he informed me that Moll White was dead; and

JOSEPH ADDISON

that about a month after her death the wind
was so very high, that it blew down the end
of one of his barns. But for my own part,
says Sir Roger, I do not think that the old
woman had any hand in it.

He afterwards fell into an account of the
diversions which had passed in his house
during the holidays; for Sir Roger, after the
laudable custom of his ancestors, always
keeps open house at Christmas. I learned
from him that he had killed eight fat hogs
for the season, that he had dealt about his
chines very liberally amongst his neighbours,
and that in particular he had sent a string
of hogs'-puddings with a pack of cards to
every poor family in the parish. I have often
thought, says Sir Roger, it happens very well
that Christmas should fall out in the middle
of the winter. It is the most dead uncomfortable time of the year, when the poor people
would suffer very much from their poverty and
cold, if they had not good cheer, warm fires,
and Christmas gambols to support them. I
love to rejoice their poor hearts at this season,
and to see the whole village merry in my
great hall. I allow a double quantity of malt
to my small beer, and set it a-running for
twelve days to every one that calls for it. I
have always a piece of cold beef and a mince-
pie upon the table, and am wonderfully pleased
to see my tenants pass away a whole evening
in playing their innocent tricks, and smutting

one another. Our friend Will Wimble is as merry as any of them, and shows a thousand roguish tricks upon these occasions.

I was very much delighted with the reflection of my old friend, which carried so much goodness in it. He then launched out into the praise of the late Act of Parliament for securing the Church of England, and told me, with great satisfaction, that he believed it already began to take effect, for that a rigid Dissenter, who chanced to dine at his house on Christmas Day, had been observed to eat very plentifully of his plum-porridge.

After having dispatched all our country matters, Sir Roger made several inquiries concerning the Club, and particularly of his old antagonist Sir Andrew Freeport. He asked me with a kind of smile, whether Sir Andrew had not taken advantage of his absence, to vent among them some of his republican doctrines; but soon after gathering up his countenance into a more than ordinary seriousness, Tell me truly, says he, don't you think Sir Andrew had a hand in the Pope's procession——but without giving me time to answer him, Well, well, says he, I know you are a wary man, and do not care to talk of public matters.

The Knight then asked me, if I had seen Prince Eugenio, and made me promise to get him a stand in some convenient place where he might have a full sight of that extraordinary man, whose presence does so much honour to the British nation. He dwelt very long on the praises of this great general, and I found that since I was with him in the country he had drawn many observations together out of his reading in 'Baker's Chronicle,' and other authors, who always lie in his hall window, which very much redound to the honour of this prince.

Having passed away the greatest part of the morning in hearing the Knight's reflections, which were partly private, and partly political, he asked me if I would smoke a pipe with him over a dish of coffee at Squire's. As I love the old man, I take delight in complying with everything that is agreeable to him, and accordingly waited on him to the coffee-house, where his venerable figure drew upon us the eyes of the whole room. He had no sooner seated himself at the upper end of the high table, but he called for a clean pipe, a paper of tobacco, a dish of coffee, a wax-candle, and the 'Supplement,' with such an air of cheerfulness and good-humour, that all the boys in the coffee-room (who seemed to take pleasure in serving him) were at once employed on his several errands, insomuch that nobody else could come at a dish of tea, till the Knight had got all his conveniences about him.

JOSEPH ADDISON

('Spectator,' No. 329.)

My friend Sir Roger de Coverley told me t'other night that he had been reading my paper upon 'Westminster Abbey,' in which, says he, there are a great many ingenious fancies. He told me, at the same time, that he observed I had promised another paper upon 'the Tombs,' and that he should be glad to go and see them with me, not having visited them since he had read history. I could not at first imagine how this came into the Knight's head, till I recollected that he had been very busy all last summer upon 'Baker's Chronicle,' which he has quoted several times in his disputes with Sir Andrew Freeport since his last coming to town. Accordingly I promised to call upon him the next morning, that we might go together to the Abbey.

I found the Knight under his butler's hands, who always shaves him. He was no sooner dressed, than he called for a glass of the Widow Trueby's water, which he told me he always drank before he went abroad. He recommended me to a dram of it at the same time, with so much heartiness, that I could not forbear drinking it. As soon as I had got it down, I found it very unpalatable; upon which the Knight observing that I had made several wry faces, told me that he knew

I should not like it at first, but that it was the best thing in the world against the stone or gravel.

I could have wished indeed that he had acquainted me with the virtues of it sooner; but it was too late to complain, and I knew what he had done was out of good-will. Sir Roger told me further, that he looked upon it to be very good for a man whilst he stayed in town, to keep off infection, and that he got together a quantity of it upon the first news of the sickness being at Dantzic: When of a sudden, turning short to one of his servants who stood behind him, he bid him call a hackney-coach, and take care it was an elderly man that drove it.

He then resumed his discourse upon Mrs. Trueby's water, telling me that the Widow Trueby was one who did more good than all the doctors and apothecaries in the county: that she distilled every poppy that grew within five miles of her; that she distributed her water gratis among all sorts of people; to which the Knight added, that she had a very great jointure, and that the whole country would fain have it a match between him and her; and truly, says Sir Roger, if I had not been engaged, perhaps I could not have done better.

His discourse was broken off by his man's telling him he had called a coach. Upon our going to it, after having cast his eye upon the wheels, he asked the coachman if his axle-tree was good; upon the fellow's telling him he would warrant it, the Knight turned to me, told me he looked like an honest man, and went in without further ceremony.

We had not gone far, when Sir Roger popping out his head, called the coachman down from his box, and upon his presenting himself at the window, asked him if he smoked; as I was considering what this would end in, he bid him stop by the way at any good tobacconist's, and take in a roll of their best Virginia. Nothing material happened in the remaining part of our journey, till we were set down at the west-end of the Abbey.

As we went up the body of the church, the Knight pointed at the trophies upon one of the new monuments, and cried out, 'A brave man, I warrant him!' Passing afterwards by Sir Cloudesley Shovel, he flung his hand that way, and cried, 'Sir Cloudesley Shovel! a very gallant man!' As we stood before Busby's tomb, the Knight uttered himself again after the same manner, 'Dr. Busby, a great man! he whipped my grandfather; a very great man! I should have gone to him myself, if I had not been a blockhead: a very great man!'

We were immediately conducted into the little chapel on the right hand. Sir Roger planting himself at our historian's elbow, was very attentive to everything he said, particu-

larly to the account he gave us of the lord
who had cut off the King of Morocco's head.
Among several other figures, he was very
well pleased to see the statesman Cecil upon
his knees; and, concluding them all to be
great men, was conducted to the figure which
represents that martyr to good housewifery,
who died by the prick of a needle. Upon our
interpreter's telling us that she was a maid
of honour to Queen Elizabeth, the Knight
was very inquisitive into her name and
family; and after having regarded her finger
for some time, I wonder, says he, that Sir
Richard Baker has said nothing of her in his
'Chronicle.'

We were then conveyed to the two coronation chairs, where my old friend, after having
heard that the stone underneath the most
ancient of them, which was brought from
Scotland, was called Jacob's Pillar, sat himself down in the chair, and looking like the
figure of an old Gothic king, asked our
interpreter what authority they had to say
that Jacob had ever been in Scotland? The
fellow, instead of returning him an answer,
told him that he hoped his honour would pay
his forfeit. I could observe Sir Roger a little
ruffled upon being thus trepanned; but our
guide not insisting upon his demand, the
Knight soon recovered his good-humour, and
whispered in my ear, that if Will Wimble
were with us, and saw those two chairs, it

would go hard but he would get a tobacco-stopper out of one or t' other of them.

Sir Roger, in the next place, laid his hand upon Edward the Third's sword, and leaning upon the pummel of it, gave us the whole history of the Black Prince; concluding, that in Sir Richard Baker's opinion, Edward the Third was one of the greatest princes that ever sat upon the English throne.

We were then shown Edward the Confessor's tomb; upon which Sir Roger acquainted us, that he was the first who touched for the evil; and afterwards Henry the Fourth's, upon which he shook his head, and told us there was fine reading in the casualties in that reign.

Our conductor then pointed to that monument where there is the figure of one of our English kings without a head; and upon giving us to know, that the head, which was of beaten silver, had been stolen away several years since: Some Whig, I'll warrant you, says Sir Roger; you ought to lock up your kings better; they will carry off the body too, if you don't take care.

The glorious names of Henry the Fifth and Queen Elizabeth gave the Knight great opportunities of shining, and of doing justice to Sir Richard Baker, who, as our Knight observed with some surprise, had a great many kings in him, whose monuments he had not seen in the Abbey.

For my own part, I could not but be
pleased to see the Knight show such an
honest passion for the glory of his country,
and such a respectful gratitude to the memory
of its princes.

I must not omit, that the benevolence of
my good old friend, which flows out towards
every one he converses with, made him very
kind to our interpreter, whom he looked upon
as an extraordinary man; for which reason
he shook him by the hand at parting, telling
him that he should be very glad to see him at
his lodgings in Norfolk Buildings, and talk
over these matters with him more at leisure.

('Spectator,' No. 335.)

My friend Sir Roger de Coverley, when we
last met together at the Club, told me that he
had a great mind to see the new Tragedy
with me, assuring me at the same time that
he had not been at a play these twenty years.
The last I saw, said Sir Roger, was the
'Committee,' which I should not have gone
to neither, had not I been told beforehand
that it was a good Church of England comedy.
He then proceeded to enquire of me who this
distressed mother was; and upon hearing
that she was Hector's widow, he told me
that her husband was a brave man, and that
when he was a school-boy he had read his life

at the end of the dictionary. My friend asked
me, in the next place, if there would not be
some danger in coming home late, in case the
Mohocks should be abroad. I assure you,
says he, I thought I had fallen into their
hands last night; for I observed two or three
lusty black men that followed me half way up
Fleet Street, and mended their pace behind
me, in proportion as I put on to get away
from them. You must know, continued the
Knight with a smile, I fancied they had a
mind to hunt me; for I remember an honest
gentleman in my neighbourhood, who was
served such a trick in King Charles the
Second's time; for which reason he has not
ventured himself in town ever since. I might
have shown them very good sport, had this
been their design; for as I am an old fox-
hunter, I should have turned and dodged, and
have played them a thousand tricks they had
never seen in their lives before. Sir Roger
added that if these gentlemen had any such
intention, they did not succeed very well in it:
for I threw them out, says he, at the end of
Norfolk Street, where I doubled the corner,
and got shelter in my lodgings before they
could imagine what was become of me.
However, says the Knight, if Captain Sentry
will make one with us to-morrow night, and
if you will both of you call upon me about
four o'clock, that we may be at the house
before it is full, I will have my own coach in

readiness to attend you, for John tells me he
has got the fore-wheels mended.

The Captain, who did not fail to meet me
there at the appointed hour, bid Sir Roger
fear nothing, for that he had put on the same
sword which he made use of at the Battle of
Steenkirk. Sir Roger's servants, and among
the rest my old friend the butler, had, I found,
provided themselves with good oaken plants,
to attend their master upon this occasion.
When he had placed him in his coach, with
myself at his left hand, the Captain before
him, and his butler at the head of his footmen
in the rear, we convoyed him in safety to the
play-house, where, after having marched up
the entry in good order, the Captain and I
went in with him, and seated him betwixt us
in the pit. As soon as the house was full, and
the candles lighted, my old friend stood up
and looked about him with that pleasure,
which a mind seasoned with humanity naturally feels in itself, at the sight of a multitude
of people who seem pleased with one another,
and partake of the same common entertainment. I could not but fancy to myself, as the
old man stood up in the middle of the pit, that
he made a very proper centre to a tragic
audience. Upon the entering of Pyrrhus,
the Knight told me that he did not believe
the King of France himself had a better strut.
I was indeed very attentive to my old friend's
remarks, because I looked upon them as a

piece of natural criticism, and was well pleased
to hear him at the conclusion of almost every
scene, telling me that he could not imagine
how the play would end. One while he
appeared much concerned for Andromache;
and a little while after as much for Hermione;
and was extremely puzzled to think what
would become of Pyrrhus.

When Sir Roger saw Andromache's obsti-
nate refusal to her lover's importunities, he
whispered me in the ear, that he was sure
she would never have him; to which he
added, with a more than ordinary vehemence,
You can't imagine, sir, what 'tis to have to
do with a widow. Upon Pyrrhus his threaten-
ing afterwards to leave her, the Knight shook
his head, and muttered to himself, Ay, do if
you can. This part dwelt so much upon my
friend's imagination, that at the close of the
third act, as I was thinking of something
else, he whispered in my ear, These widows,
sir, are the most perverse creatures in the
world. But pray, says he, you that are a critic,
is this play according to your dramatic rules,
as you call them? Should your people in
tragedy always talk to be understood? Why,
there is not a single sentence in this play that
I do not know the meaning of.

The fourth act very luckily begun before
I had time to give the old gentleman an
answer: Well, says the Knight, sitting down
with great satisfaction, I suppose we are

now to see Hector's Ghost. He then renewed his attention, and, trom time to time, fell a praising the widow. He made, indeed, a little mistake as to one of her pages, whom at his first entering, he took for Astyanax; but he quickly set himself right in that particular, though at the same time, he owned he should have been very glad to have seen the little boy, who, says he, must needs be a very fine child by the account that is given of him. Upon Hermione's going off with a menace to Pyrrhus, the audience gave a loud clap; to which Sir Roger added, On my word, a notable young baggage!

As there was a very remarkable silence and stillness in the audience during the whole action, it was natural for them to take the opportunity of these intervals between the acts, to express their opinion of the players, and of their respective parts. Sir Roger hearing a cluster of them praise Orestes, struck in with them, and told them that he thought his friend Pylades was a very sensible man; as they were afterwards applauding Pyrrhus, Sir Roger put in a second time: And let me tell you, says he, though he speaks but little, I like the old fellow in whiskers as well as any of them. Captain Sentry seeing two or three wags who sat near us, lean with an attentive ear towards Sir Roger, and fearing lest they should smoke the Knight, plucked him by the elbow.

and whispered something in his ear, that lasted till the opening of the fifth act. The Knight was wonderfully attentive to the account which Orestes gives of Pyrrhus his death, and at the conclusion of it, told me it was such a bloody piece of work, that he was glad it was not done upon the stage. Seeing afterwards Orestes in his raving fit, he grew more than ordinary serious, and took occasion to moralise (in his way) upon an evil conscience, adding, that Orestes in his madness, looked as if he saw something.

As we were the first that came into the house, so we were the last that went out of it; being resolved to have a clear passage for our old friend, whom we did not care to venture among the justling of the crowd. Sir Roger went out fully satisfied with his entertainment, and we guarded him to his lodgings in the same manner that we brought him to the playhouse; being highly pleased, for my own part, not only with the performance of the excellent piece which had been presented, but with the satisfaction which it had given to the good old man.

('Spectator,' No. 383.)

As I was sitting in my chamber, and thinking on a subject for my next 'Spectator,' I heard two or three irregular bounces at my landlady's door, and upon the opening of it, a loud cheerful voice enquiring whether the philosopher was at home. The child who went to the door answered very innocently, that he did not lodge there. I immediately recollected that it was my good friend Sir Roger's voice; and that I had promised to go with him on the water to Spring Garden, in case it proved a good evening. The Knight put me in mind of my promise from the bottom of the staircase, but told me that if I was speculating he would stay below till I had done. Upon my coming down, I found all the children of the family got about my old friend, and my landlady herself, who is a notable prating gossip, engaged in a conference with him; being mightily pleased with his stroking her little boy upon the head, and bidding him be a good child and mind his book.

We were no sooner come to the Temple Stairs, but we were surrounded with a crowd of watermen, offering us their respective services. Sir Roger, after having looked about him very attentively, spied one with a wooden-leg, and immediately gave him orders to get his boat ready. As we were walking towards it, 'You must know,' says Sir Roger, 'I never make use of anybody to row me, that has not either lost a leg or an arm. I would rather bate him a few strokes of his oar, than not employ an honest man that has been wounded in the Queen's service. If I was a lord or a bishop, and kept a barge, I would not put a fellow in my livery that had not a wooden-leg.'

My old friend, after having seated himself, and trimmed the boat with his coachman, who being a very sober man, always serves for ballast on these occasions, we made the best of our way for Fox Hall. Sir Roger obliged the waterman to give us the history of his right leg, and hearing that he had left it at La Hogue, with many particulars which passed in that glorious action, the Knight in the triumph of his heart made several reflections on the greatness of the British nation; as, that one Englishman could beat three Frenchmen; that we could never be in danger of Popery so long as we took care of our fleet; that the Thames was the noblest river in Europe; that London Bridge was a greater piece of work than any of the seven wonders of the world; with many other honest prejudices which naturally cleave to the heart of a true Englishman.

After some short pause, the old Knight turning about his head twice or thrice, to take a survey of this great Metropolis, bid me observe how thick the City was set with churches, and that there was scarce a single steeple on this side Temple Bar. 'A most heathenish sight!' says Sir Roger; 'There is no religion at this end of the town. The fifty new churches will very much mend the prospect; but church work is slow, church work is slow!'

I do not remember I have anywhere mentioned, in Sir Roger's character, his custom of saluting everybody that passes by him with a good-morrow or a good-night. This the old man does out of the overflowings of his humanity, though at the same time it renders him so popular among all his country neighbours, that it is thought to have gone a good way in making him once or twice Knight of the Shire. He cannot forbear this exercise of benevolence even in town, when he meets with any one in his morning or evening walk. It broke from him to several boats that passed by us upon the water; but to the Knight's great surprise, as he gave the good-night to two or three young fellows a little before our landing, one of them, instead of returning the civility, asked us what queer old put we had in the boat, and whether he was not ashamed to go a wenching at his years? with a great deal of the like Thames ribaldry. Sir Roger seemed a little shocked at first, but at length assuming a face of magistracy, told us, 'That if he were a Middlesex justice, he would make such vagrants know that Her Majesty's subjects were no more to be abused by water than by land.'

We were now arrived at Spring Garden, which is exquisitely pleasant at this time of

year. When I considered the fragrancy of
the walks and bowers, with the choirs of birds
that sung upon the trees, and the loose tribe
of people that walked under the shades, I
could not but look upon the place as a kind
of Mahometan paradise. Sir Roger told me
it put him in mind of a little coppice by his
house in the country, which his chaplain
used to call an aviary of nightingales. 'You
must understand,' says the Knight, 'there is
nothing in the world that pleases a man in
love so much as your nightingale. Ah, Mr.
Spectator, the many moonlight nights that
I have walked by myself, and thought on the
Widow by the music of the nightingales!'
He here fetched a deep sigh, and was falling
into a fit of musing, when a masque who
came behind him, gave him a gentle tap upon
the shoulder, and asked him if he would drink
a bottle of mead with her? But the Knight,
being startled at so unexpected a familiarity, and displeased to be interrupted in his
thoughts of the Widow, told her, 'She was
a wanton baggage,' and bid her go about her
business.

We concluded our walk with a glass of
Burton-ale, and a slice of hung-beef. When
we had done eating ourselves, the Knight
called a waiter to him, and bid him carry the
remainder to the waterman that had but one
leg. I perceived the fellow stared upon him
at the oddness of the message, and was

going to be saucy: upon which I ratified the Knight's commands with a peremptory look.

As we were going out of the garden, my old friend, thinking himself obliged, as a member of the Quorum, to animadvert upon the morals of the place, told the mistress of the house, who sat at the bar, That he should be a better customer to her garden, if there were more nightingales and fewer strumpets.

('Spectator,' No. 517.)

We last night received a piece of ill news at our club, which very sensibly afflicted every one of us. I question not but my readers themselves will be troubled at the hearing of it. To keep them no longer in suspense, Sir Roger de Coverley is dead. He departed this life at his house in the country, after a few weeks' sickness. Sir Andrew Freeport has a letter from one of his correspondents in those parts, that informs him the old man caught a cold at the County Sessions, as he was very warmly promoting an address of his own penning, in which he succeeded according to his wishes. But this particular comes from a Whig Justice of Peace, who was always Sir Roger's enemy and antagonist. I have letters both from the chaplain and Captain Sentry which mention nothing of it, but are filled with many particulars to the honour of

the good old man. I have likewise a letter
from the butler, who took so much care of
me last summer when I was at the Knight's
house. As my friend the butler mentions, in
the simplicity of his heart, several circumstances the others have passed over in silence,
I shall give my reader a copy of his letter,
without any alteration or diminution :

'Honoured Sir,—Knowing that you was my
old master's good friend, I could not forbear
sending you the melancholy news of his death,
which has afflicted the whole country, as well
as his poor servants, who loved him, I may
say, better than we did our lives. I am afraid
he caught his death the last County Sessions,
where he would go to see justice done to a
poor widow woman, and her fatherless children, that had been wronged by a neighbouring gentleman ; for, you know, Sir, my
good master was always the poor man's
friend. Upon his coming home, the first
complaint he made was, that he had lost his
roast-beef stomach, not being able to touch a
sirloin, which was served up according to
custom ; and you know he used to take great
delight in it. From that time forward he
grew worse and worse, but still kept a good
heart to the last. Indeed we were once in
great hope of his recovery, upon a kind message that was sent him from the widow lady
whom he had made love to the forty last

years of his life; but this only proved a
lightening before death. He has bequeathed
to this lady, as a token of his love, a great
pearl necklace, and a couple of silver bracelets
set with jewels, which belonged to my good
old lady his mother: he has bequeathed the
fine white gelding, that he used to ride a
hunting upon, to his chaplain, because he
thought he would be kind to him, and has left
you all his books. He has, moreover, bequeathed to the chaplain a very pretty tene-
ment with good lands about it. It being a
very cold day when he made his will, he left
for mourning, to every man in the parish, a
great frize-coat, and to every woman a black
riding-hood. It was a most moving sight to
see him take leave of his poor servants, commending us all for our fidelity, whilst we were
not able to speak a word for weeping. As
we most of us are grown grey-headed in our
dear master's service, he has left us pensions
and legacies, which we may live very com-
fortably upon, the remaining part of our days.
He has bequeathed a great deal more in
charity, which is not yet come to my knowledge, and it is peremptorily said in the parish,
that he has left money to build a steeple to the
church; for he was heard to say some time
ago, that if he lived two years longer, Coverley
Church should have a steeple to it. The chaplain tells everybody that he made a very good
end, and never speaks of him without tears.

He was buried according to his own directions, among the family of the Coverleys, on the left hand of his father Sir Arthur. The coffin was carried by six of his tenants, and the pall held up by six of the quorum: the whole parish followed the corps with heavy hearts, and in their mourning suits, the men in frize, and the women in riding-hoods. Captain Sentry, my master's nephew, has taken possession of the Hall-house, and the whole estate. When my old master saw him a little before his death, he shook him by the hand, and wished him joy of the estate which was falling to him, desiring him only to make good use of it, and to pay the several legacies, and the gifts of charity which he told him he had left as quit-rents upon the estate. The Captain truly seems a courteous man, though he says but little. He makes much of those whom my master loved, and shows great kindness to the old house-dog, that you know my poor master was so fond of. It would have gone to your heart to have heard the moans the dumb creature made on the day of my master's death. He has ne'er joyed himself since; no more has any of us. 'Twas the melancholiest day for the poor people that ever happened in Worcestershire. This being all from,—Honoured Sir, your most sorrowful servant, Edward Biscuit.'

'P.S.—My master desired, some weeks

before he died, that a book which comes up
to you by the carrier should be given to Sir
Andrew Freeport, in his name.'

This letter, notwithstanding the poor butler's manner of writing it, gave us such an
idea of our good old friend, that upon the
reading of it there was not a dry eye in the
club. Sir Andrew opening the book, found
it to be a collection of Acts of Parliament.
There was in particular the Act of Uniformity,
with some passages in it marked by Sir
Roger's own hand. Sir Andrew found that
they related to two or three points, which he
had disputed with Sir Roger the last time he
appeared at the club. Sir Andrew, who
would have been merry at such an incident
on another occasion, at the sight of the old
man's handwriting burst into tears, and put
the book into his pocket. Captain Sentry
informs me, that the Knight has left rings and
mourning for every one in the club.

RICHARD STEELE

ESSAYS FROM 'THE LOVER'

No. I.—Thursday, February 25, 1714.

'Virginibus Puerisque Canto.'—Hor.

There have been many and laudable en-
deavours of late years, by sundry authors,
under different characters, and of different

inclinations and capacities, to improve the world, by half-sheet advertisements, in learning, wit, and politics; but these works have not attentively enough regarded the softer affections of the mind, which being properly raised and awakened, make way for the operation of all good arts.

After mature deliberation with myself upon this subject, I have thought, that if I could trace the passion or affection of love, through all its joys and inquietudes, through all the stages and circumstances of life, in both sexes, with strict respect to virtue and innocence, I should, by a just representation and history of that one passion, steal into the bosom of my reader, and build upon it all the sentiments and resolutions which incline and qualify us for everything that is truly excellent, great, and noble.

All you, therefore, who are in the dawn of life, as to conversation with a faithless and artful world, attend to one who has passed through almost all the mazes of it, and is familiarly acquainted with whatever can befall you in the pursuit of love: If you diligently observe me, I will teach you to avoid the temptations of lawless desire, which leads to shame and sorrow, and carry you into the paths of love, which will conduct you to honour and happiness. This passion is the source of our being, and as it is so, it is also the support of it; for all the adventures which

195

they meet with who swerve from love, carry them so far out of the way of their true being, which cannot pleasingly pass on when it has deviated from the rules of honourable passion.

My purpose therefore, under this title, is to write of such things only which ought to please all men, even as men ; and I shall never hope for prevailing under this character of 'Lover' from my force in the reason offered, but as that reason makes for the happiness and satisfaction of the person to whom I address. My reader is to be my mistress, and I shall always endeavour to turn my thoughts so as that there shall be nothing in my writings too severe to be spoken before one unacquainted with learning, or too light to be dwelt upon before one who is either fixed already in the paths of virtue, or desirous to walk in them for the future.

My assistants, in this work, are persons whose conduct of life has turned upon the incidents which have occurred to them from this agreeable or lamentable passion, as they respectively are apt to call it, from the impression it has left upon their imaginations, and which mingles in all their words and actions.

It cannot be supposed the gentlemen can be called by their real names, in so public a manner as this is. But the hero of my story, now in the full bloom of life, and seen every day in all the places of resort, shall bear the

name of one of our British rivers, which
washes his estate. As I design this paper
shall be a picture of familiar life, I shall avoid
words derived from learned languages, or
ending in foreign terminations: I shall shun
also names significant of the person's character of whom I talk ; a trick used by play-
wrights, which I have long thought no better
a device than that of underwriting the name
of an animal on a post, which the painter
conceived too delicately drawn to be known
by common eyes, or by his delineation of its
limbs.

Mr. Severn is now in the twenty-fifth year
of his age, a gentleman of great modesty and
courage, which are the radical virtues which
lay the solid foundation for a good character
and behaviour both in public and private. I
will not, at this time, make the reader any
further acquainted with him than from this
particular, that he extremely affects the conversation of people of merit who are advanced
in years, and treats every woman of condition,
who is past being entertained on the foot of
homage to her beauty, so respectfully, that in
his company she can never give herself the
compunction of having lost anything which
made her agreeable. This natural goodness
has gained him many hearts, which have
agreeable persons to give with them : I mean,
mothers have a fondness for him, and with
that fondness, could be gratified by his pas-

sion to their daughters. Were you to visit him in the morning, you would certainly find some awkward thing of business, some old steward, or distant retainer to a great family, who has a proposal to make to him, not (you may be sure) coming from the person who sent him, but only in general to know whether he is engaged.

Mr. Severn has at this time patterns sent him of all the young women in town; and I, who am of his council in these matters, have read his particulars of women brought him, not from professed undertakers that way, but from those who are under no necessity of selling immediately, but such who have daughters a good way under twenty, that can stay for a market, and send in their account of the lady, in general terms only; as that she is so old, so tall, worth so much down, and has two bachelor uncles (one a rich merchant) that will never marry; her maiden aunt loves her mightily, and has very fine jewels, and the like. I have observed in these accounts, when the fortune is not suitable, they subjoin a postscript, she is very handsome; if she is rich and defective as to charms, they add, she is very good.

But I was going to say, that Mr. Severn having the good sense to affect the conversation of those elder than himself, passes some time at a club, which (with himself) consists of six; whom we shall name as follows.

Mr. Oswald, a widower, who has within these few months buried a most agreeable woman, who was his beloved wife, and is indulged by this company to speak of her in the terms she deserved of him, with allowance to mingle family-tales concerning the merit of his children, and the ways and methods he designs to take, to support a painful and lonely being, after the loss of this companion, which tempered all his sorrows, and gave new sense and spirit to his satisfactions.

Mr. Mullet, a gentleman, who in the most plentiful fortune, seems to taste very little of life, because he has lost a lady whom he passionately loved, and by whom he had no children ; he is the last of a great house, and though he wants not many months of fifty, is much sought by ladies as bright as any of the sex ; but as he is no fool, but is sensible, they compare his years with their own, and have a mind to marry him, because they have a mind to bury him, he is as froward, exceptious, and humoursome as e'er a beauty of 'em all : I, who am intimate with Mullet as well as Severn, know that many of the same women have been offered to him of fifty, in case of losing him of five and twenty ; and some perhaps in hopes of having them both : for they prudently judge, that when Mullet is dead, it may then be time enough for Severn to marry ; and a lady's-maid can observe that

many an unlikelier thing has come to pass,
than this view of marriage between her young
mistress and both those gentlemen.

Mr. Johnson is a gentleman happy in the
conversation of an excellent wife, by whom
he has a numerous offspring ; and the manner
of subjecting his desires to his circumstances,
which are not too plentiful, may give occasion
in my future discourses to draw many incidents
of domestic life, which may be as agreeable to
the rest of the young men of this nation, as
they are to the well-disposed Mr. Severn.

The fifth man of this little assembly is
Mr. Wildgoose, an old bachelor, who has
lived to the fifty-third year of his age, after
being disappointed in love at his twenty-third.
That torment of mind frets out in little dis-
satisfactions and uneasinesses against everything else, without administering remedy to
the ail itself, which still festers in his heart,
and would be insupportable, were it not
cooled by the society of the others above
mentioned. A poor old maid is one, who
has long been the object of ridicule, her
humours and particularities afford much matter
to the facetious ; but the old bachelor has
ten times more of the splenetic and ridiculous,
as he is conversant in larger scenes of life,
and has more opportunities to diffuse his folly,
and consequently can vex and delight people
in more views, than an ancient virgin of the
other sex.

The sixth and last of this company, is my dear self, who oblige the world with this work. But as it has been frequently observed, that the fine gentleman of a play has always something in him which is of near alliance to the real character of the author, I shall not pretend to be wholly above that pleasure, but shall in the next paper principally talk of myself, and satisfy my readers how well I am qualified to be the secretary of love. I had ordered my bookseller to adorn the head of my paper with little pretty broken arrows, fans thrown away, and other ensigns armorial of the Isle of Paphos, for the embellishment of my work ; but as I am a young author, and pretend to no more but a happy imitation of one who went before me, he would not be at that charge ; when I failed there, I desired him only to let the paper be gilded ; but he said that was a new thing, and it would be taken to be written by a person of quality, which, I know not for what reason, the bibliopoles are also very averse to, and I was denied my second request. However, this did not discourage me, and I was resolved to come out ; not without some particular hopes, that if I had not so many admirers, I might possibly have more customers than my predecessor, whom I profess to imitate ; for there are many more who can feel what will touch the heart, than receive what would improve the head.

I therefore design to be the comfort and consolation of all persons in a languishing condition, and will receive the complaints of all the faithful sighers in city, town, or country; firmly believing, that as bad as the world is, there are as constant ones within the cities of London and Westminster, as ever wandered in the plains of Arcadia.

I shall in my next paper (as much as I can spare of it, from talking of myself) tell the world how to communicate their thoughts to me, which will very properly come in with the description of my apartment, and the furniture of it, together with the account of my person, which shall make up the second paper or chapter, and shall be placed before the Errata of this. I have nothing further to say now, but am willing to make an end of this leaf as quaintly as possible, being the first; and therefore would have it go off like an act in a play, with a couplet; but the spirit of that will be wholly in the power of the reader, who must quicken his voice hereabouts, like an actor at his exit, helping an empty verse with lively hand, foot, and voice, at once, ; and if he is reading to ladies, say briskly, that, with regard to the greatest part of mankind,

> Foreign is every character beside ;
> But that of lover every man has try'd.

No. 3.—Tuesday, March 2.

Young nobles, to my laws attention lend:
And all you vulgar of my school, attend.
        ' Art of Love,' Congreve.

Lover's-Lodge, March 2.

Now I have told all the world my name
and place of abode, it is impossible for me
to enjoy the studious retirement I promised
myself in this place. For most of the people
of wit and quality who frequented these
lodgings in Mr. Powell's time, have been
here, and I having a silly creature of a footman who never lived but with private gentlemen, and cannot steadfastly lie, they all see
by his countenance he does not speak truth
when he denies me, and will break in upon
me. It is an unspeakable pleasure that so
many beauteous ladies have made me compli-
ments upon my design to favour and defend
the sex against all pretenders without merit,
and those who have merit, and use it only to
deceive and betray. The principal fair ones
of the town, and the most eminent toasts,
have signed an address of thanks to me,
and in the body of it laid before me some
grievances, among which the greatest are
the evil practices of a set of persons whom
they call in their presentation the Lover
Vagabond. There has been indeed, ever
since I knew this town, one man of condition

or other, who has been at the head, and,
giving example to this sort of companions,
been the model for the fashion.   It would
be a vain thing to pretend to property in a
country where thieves were tolerated, and
it is as much so to talk of honour and
decency when the prevailing humour runs
directly against them.   The Lovers Vagabond
are an order of modern adventurers, who seem
to be the exact opposite to that venerable and
chaste fraternity, which were formerly called
Knights Errant.   As a Knight Errant professed the practice and protection of all
virtues, particularly chastity, a Lover Vagabond tramples upon all rights domestic, civil,
human and divine, to come at his own
gratification in the corruption of innocent
women.   There are sometimes persons of
good accomplishments and faculties who
commence secretly Lovers Vagabond; but
tho' amorous stealths have been imputed
by some historians to the wisest and greatest
of mankind, yet none but superficial men
have ever publicly entered into the list of
the Vagabond.   A Lover Vagabond, considering him in his utmost perfection and
accomplishment, is but a seeming man.   He
usually has a command of insignificant words
accompanied with easy action, which passes
among the sillier part of the fair for eloquence
and fine breeding.   He has a mien of con-
descension, from the knowledge that his

carriage is not absurd, which he pursues to
the utmost impudence. He can cover any
behaviour, or clothe any idea with words
that to an unskilful ear shall bear nothing of
offence. He has all the sufficiency which
little learning, and general notices of things
give to giddy heads, and is wholly exempt
from that diffidence which almost always
accompanies great sense and great virtue in
the presence of the admired. But the Lover
Vagabond loving no woman so much as to
be distressed for the loss of her, his manner is
generally easy and jaunty, and it must be
from very good sense and experience in life,
that he does not appear amiable. It happens
unfortunately for him, tho' much to the
advantage of those whom I have taken
under my care, that the chief of this order,
at present, among us in Great Britain, is
but a speculative 'Debauchée.' He has the
language, the air, the tender glance; he can
hang upon a look, has most exactly the
sudden veneration of face when he is catched
ogling one whose pardon he would beg for
gazing, he has the exultation at leading off
a lady to her coach; can let drop an indifferent thing, or call her servants with a
loudness, and a certain gay insolence well
enough; nay, he will hold her hand too fast
for a man that leads her, and is indifferent to
her, and yet come to that gripe with such
slow degrees, that she cannot say he squeezed

her hand, but for anything further he has no inclination. This chieftain, however, I fear, will give me more plague and disturbance than any one man with whom I am to engage, or rather whom I am to circumvent. He is busy in all places; an ample fortune and vigour of life enable him to carry on a show of great devastation wherever he comes. But I give him hereby fair warning to turn his thoughts to new entertainments, upon pain of having it discovered that she is still a virgin upon whom he made his last settlement. The secret, that he is more innocent than he seems, is preserved by great charge and expense on humble retainers and servants of his pleasures. But some of the women, who are above the age of novices, have found him out, and have in a private gang given him the nickname of the Blite, for that they find themselves blasted by him, though they are not sensible of his touch. It was the other day said, at a visit, Mr. such a one, naming the Blite, had ruined a certain young lady; ' No,' said a sensible female, ' if she says so, I am sure she wrongs him. He may,' continued she, with an air of a disappointed woman, between rage and laughter, ' hire ruffians to abuse her, but many a woman has come out of the Blite's hands even safer than she wished. I know one, to whom, at parting, with a thousand poetical repetitions, and pressing

RICHARD STEELE

her hands, he vowed he would tell nobody;
but the flirt, throwing out of his arms,
answered pertly, "I don't make you the same
promise."'

Though I shall from time to time display
the Lovers Vagabond in their proper colours,
I here publish an Act of Indemnity to all
females who took them for fine fellows until
my writings appeared, that is to say (for in
a public act we must be very clear) I shall
not look back to anything that happened
before Thursday the 25th of February last
past, that being the first day of my appearance in public.

I expect, therefore, to find that on that day
all vagrant desires took their leave of the cities
of London and Westminster.

In order to recover simplicity of manners
without the loss of true gaiety of life, I shall
take upon me the office of Arbiter Elegan-
tiarum. I cannot easily put those two Latin
into two as expressive English words; but
my meaning is, to set up for a judge of
elegant pleasures, and I shall dare to assert
in the first place (to show both the discerning
and severity of a just judge), that the greatest
elegance of delights consists in the innocence
of them; I expect, therefore, a seat to be
kept for me at all balls, and a ticket sent,
that by myself, or a subordinate officer of
mine, I may know what is done and said at
all assemblies of diversion; I shall take care

207

to substitute none, where I cannot be myself present, who are not fit for the best bred society; in the choice of such deputies I shall have particular regard to their being accomplished in the little usages of ordinary and common life, as well as in noble and liberal arts.

I have many youths, who, in the intermediate seasons between the terms at the universities, are under my discipline, after being perfect masters of the Greek and Roman eloquence, to learn of me ordinary things, such as coming in, and going out of a room. Mr. Severn himself, whom I now make the pattern of good-breeding, and my top fine gentleman, was with me twice a day for six months upon his first coming to town, before he could leave the room with any tolerable grace; when he had a mind to be going he never could move without bringing in the words, 'Well, sir, I find I interrupt you'; or 'Well, I fear you have other business'; or 'Well, I must be going'; hereupon I made him give me a certain sum of money down in hand, under the penalty of forfeiting twenty shillings every time upon going away he pronounced the particle 'well.' I will not say how much it cost him before he could get well out of the room. Some silly particle or other, as it were to tack the taking leave with the rest of the discourse, is a common error of young men of good education.

208

Though I have already declared I shall not use words of foreign termination, I cannot help it if my correspondents do it. A gentleman therefore who subscribes 'Aronces,' and writes to me concerning some regulations to be made among a set of country dancers, must be more particular in his account. His general complaint is, that the men who are at the expense of the ball, bring people of different characters together, and the libertine and innocent are huddled, to the danger of the latter, and encouragement of the former. I have frequently observed this kind of enormity, and must desire 'Aronces' to give me an exact relation of the airs and glances of the whole company, and particularly how Mrs. Gatty sets, when it happens that she is to pass by the Lover Vagabond, who, I find, is got into that company by the favour of his cousin Jenny. For I design to have a very strict eye upon these diversions, and it shall not suffice, that, according to the author of 'The Rape of the Lock,' all faults are laid upon sylphs; when I make my enquiry, as the same author has it,

What guards the purity of melting maids
In courtly balls and midnight masquerades,
Safe from the treacherous friend and daring
    spark,
The glance by day and whisper in the dark?
When kind occasion prompts their warm
    desires,
When music softens, and when dancing fires?

No. 5.—Saturday, March 6

My soul's far better part,
Cease weeping, nor afflict thy tender heart,
For what thy father to thy mother was,
That faith to thee, that solemn vow I pass!
'Art of Love,' Congreve.

As I have fixed my stand in the very centre
of Covent Garden, a place for this last century
particularly famed for wit and love, and am
near the play-house, where one is represented
every night by the other, I think I ought to
be particularly careful of what passes in my
neighbourhood; and as I am a professed
knight-errant, do all that lies in my power to
make the charming endowment of wit, and
the prevailing passion of love, subservient to
the interests of honour and virtue. You are
to understand, that having yesterday made an
excursion from my lodge, there passed by me
near St. James's the charmer of my heart. I
have, ever since her parents first bestowed
her, avoided all places by her frequented; but
accident once or twice in a year brings the
bright phantom into my sight, upon which
there is a flutter in my bosom for many days
following; when I consider that during this
emotion I am highly exalted in my being,
and my every sentiment improved by the
effects of that passion; when I reflect that
all the objects which present themselves to

me, now are viewed in a different light from
that in which they had appeared, had I not
lately been exhilarated by her presence; in
fine, when I find in myself so strong an
inclination to oblige and entertain all whom
I meet with, accompanied with such a readiness to receive kind impressions of those I
converse with, I am more and more convinced, that this passion is in honest minds
the strongest incentive that can move the
soul of man to laudable accomplishments. Is
a man just? let him fall in love and grow
generous; is a man good-natured? let him
love and grow public-spirited. It immediately makes the good which is in him shine
forth in new excellences, and the ill vanish
away without the pain of contrition, but with
a sudden amendment of heart. This sort of
passion, to produce such effects, must neces-
sarily be conceived towards a modest and
virtuous woman; for the arts to obtain her
must be such as are agreeable to her, and the
lover becomes immediately possessed with
such perfections or vices, as make way to the
object of his desires. I have plenty of examples to enforce these truths, every night
that a play is acted in my neighbourhood;
the noble resolutions which heroes in tragedy
take, in order to recommend themselves to
their mistresses, are no way below the consideration of the wisest men, yet, at the same
time, instructions the most probable to take

place in the minds of the young and incon
siderate: but in our degenerate age the poet
must have more than ordinary skill to raise
the admiration of the audience so high, in the
more great and public parts of his drama, to
make a loose people attend to a passion which
they never, or that very faintly, felt in their
own bosoms. That perfect piece, which has
done so great honour to our nation and
language, called 'Cato,' excels as much in
the passion of its lovers, as in the sublime
sentiments of its hero; their generous love,
which is more heroic than any concern in the
chief characters of most dramas, makes but
subordinate characters in this.

When Marcia reproves Juba for entertain-
ing her with love in such a conjuncture of
affairs, wherein the common cause should
take place of all other thoughts, the prince
answers in this noble manner:

        Thy reproofs are just,
Thou virtuous maid; I'll hasten to my troops,
And fire their languid souls with Cato's
    virtue.
If e'er I lead them to the field, when all
The war shall stand ranged in its just array,
And dreadful pomp: then will I think on
    thee!
O lovely maid, then will I think on thee!
And in the shock of charging hosts, remember
What glorious deeds shou'd grace the man,
    who hopes
For Marcia's love.

It has been observable, that the stage in all times has had the utmost influence on the manners and affections of mankind ; and as those representations of human life have tended to promote virtue or vice, so has the age been improved or debauched. I doubt not but the frequent reflections upon marriage and innocent love, with which our theatre has long abounded, have been the great cause of our corrupt sentiments in this respect. It is not every youth that can behold the fine gentleman of the comedy represented with a good grace, leading a loose and profligate life, and condemning virtuous affection as insipid, and not be secretly emulous of what appears so amiable to a whole audience. These gay pictures strike strong and lasting impressions on the fancy and imagination of youth, and are hardly to be erased in riper years, unless a commerce between virtuous and innocent lovers be painted with the same advantage, and with as lovely colours by the most masterly hands on the theatre. I have said masterly hands, because they must be such who can run counter to our natural propensity to inordinate pleasure ; little authors are very glad of applause purchased any way ; loose appetites and desires are easily raised, but there is a wide difference between that reputation and applause which is obtained from our wantonness, and that which flows from a capacity of stirring such affections

213

which, upon cool thoughts, contribute to our happiness.

But I was going to give an account of the exultation which I am in, upon an accidental view of the woman whom I had long loved, with a most pure, tho' ardent passion; but as this is, according to my former representations of the matter, no way expedient for her to indulge me in, I must break the force of it by leading a life suitable and analogous to it, and making all the town sensible, how much they owe to her bright eyes which inspire me in the performance of my present office, in which I shall particularly take all the youth of both sexes under my care.

The two theatres, and all the polite coffee-houses, I shall constantly frequent, but principally the coffee-house under my lodge, Button's, and the play-house in Covent Garden. But as I set up for the judge of pleasures, I think it necessary to assign particular places of resort to my young gentlemen as they come to town, who cannot expect to pop in at Mr. Button's, on the first day of their arrival in town. I recommend it, therefore, to young men to frequent Shanley's some days before they take upon them to appear at Button's; I have ordered that no one look in the face of any new comer, and taken effectual methods that he may possess himself of any empty chair in the house without being stared at; but forasmuch as some

who may have been in town for some months
together heretofore, by long absence have
relapsed from the audacity they had arrived
at, into their first bashfulness and rusticity, I
have given them the same privilege of obscure
entry for ten days. I have directed also, that
books be kept of all that passes in town in all
the eminent coffee-houses, that any gentleman, though just arrived out of exile from
the most distant counties in Great Britain,
may as familiarly enter into the town-talk, as
if he had lodged all that time in Covent
Garden ; but above all things I have provided,
that proper houses for bathing and cupping
may be ready for those country gentlemen,
whose too healthy visages give them an air
too robust and importunate for this polite
region of lovers, who have so long avoided
wind and weather, and have every day been
outstripped by them in the ground they have
passed over by several miles. As to the
orders under which I have put my female
youth at assemblies, operas, and plays, I
shall declare them in a particular chapter
under the title of, 'The Government of the
Eye in Public Places.'

RICHARD STEELE

No. 7.—Thursday, March 11

'—— halet et sua castra Cupido.'—Ov.

THE BATTLE OF EYES

It has been always my opinion, that a man in love should address himself to his mistress with passion and sincerity; and that if this method fails, it is in vain for him to have recourse to artifice or dissimulation, in which he will always find himself worsted, unless he be a much better proficient in the art than any man I have yet been acquainted with.

The following letter is a very natural exemplification of what I have here advanced. I have called it 'The Battle of Eyes,' as it brought to my mind several combats of the same nature, which I have formerly had with Mrs. Ann Page.

'Sweet Mr. Myrtle,—I have for some time been sorely smitten by Mrs. Lucy, who is a maiden lady in the twenty-eighth year of her age. She has so much of the coquette in her, that it supplies the place of youth, and still keeps up the girl in her aspect and behaviour. She has found out the art of making me believe that I have the first place in her affection, and yet so puzzles me by a double tongue, and an ambiguous look, that about once a fortnight I fancy I have quite lost her.

216

I was the other night at the Opera, where seeing a place in the second row of the Queen's Box kept by Mrs. Lucy's livery, I placed myself in the pit directly over against her footman, being determined to ogle her most passionately all that evening. I had not taken my stand there above a quarter of an hour, when enter Mrs. Lucy. At her first coming in I expected she would have cast her eye upon her humble servant; but, instead of that, after having dropped curtsey after curtsey to her friends in the boxes, she began to deal her salutes about the pit in the same liberal manner. Although I stood in the full point of view, and, as I thought, made a better figure than anybody about me, she slid her eye over me, curtseyed to the right and to the left, and would not see me for the space of three minutes. I fretted inwardly to find myself thus openly affronted on every side, and was resolved to let her know my resentments by the first opportunity. This happened soon after; for Mrs. Lucy looking upon me, as though she had but just discovered me, she begun to sink in the first offer to a curtsey; upon which, instead of making her any return, I cocked my nose, and stared at the upper gallery; and immediately after raising myself on tiptoe, stretched out my neck, and bowed to a lady who sat just behind her. I found, by my coquette's behaviour, that she was not a little nettled at this my civility,

which passed over her head. She looked as
pale as ashes, fell a-talking with one that sat
next her, and broke out into several forced
smiles and fits of laughter, which I dare say
there was no manner of occasion for. Being
resolved to push my success, I cast my eye
through the whole circle of beauties, and
made my bow to every one that I knew, and
to several whom I never saw before in my
life. Things were thus come to an open rup-
ture, when the curtain rising, I was forced to
face about. I had not sat down long, but my
heart relented, and gave me several girds and
twitches for the barbarous treatment which I
had shown to Mrs. Lucy. I longed to see the
act ended, and to make reparation for what I
had done. At the first rising of the audience,
between the acts, our eyes met; but as mine
begun to offer a parley, the hard-hearted slut
conveyed herself behind an old lady in such
a manner, that she was concealed from me for
several moments. This gave me new matter
of indignation, and I begun to fancy I had lost
her for ever. While I was in this perplexity
of thought, Mrs. Lucy lifted herself up from
behind the lady who shadowed her, and
peeped at me over her right shoulder. Nay,
madam, thinks I to myself, if those are your
tricks, I will give you as good as you bring;
upon which I withdrew, in a great passion,
behind a tall broad-shouldered fellow, who
was very luckily placed before me. I here lay

incog. for at least three seconds; snug was
the word; but being very uneasy in that
situation, I again emerged into open candle-
light, when looking for Mrs. Lucy, I could
see nothing but the old woman, who screened
her for the remaining part of the interlude. I
was then forced to sit down to the second
act, being very much agitated and tormented
in mind. I was terribly afraid that she had
discovered my uneasiness, as well knowing,
that if she caught me at such an advantage,
she would use me like a dog. For this reason
I was resolved to play the indifferent upon her
at my next standing up. The second act,
therefore, was no sooner finished, but I
fastened my eye upon a young woman who
sat at the further end of the boxes, whispering
at the same time, to one who was near me,
with an air of pleasure and admiration. I
gazed upon her a long time, when stealing a
glance at Mrs. Lucy, with a design to see
how she took it, I found her face was turned
another way, and that she was examining,
from head to foot, a young well-dressed rascal
who stood behind her. This cut me to the
quick, and notwithstanding I tossed back my
wig, rapped my snuff-box, displayed my hand-
kerchief, and at last cracked a jest with an
orange wench, to attract her eye, she per-
sisted in her confounded ogle, till Mrs. Robin-
son came upon the stage to my relief. I now
sat down sufficiently mortified, and deter-

mined, at the end of the opera, to make my
submission in the most humble manner. Accordingly, rising up, I put on a sneaking
penitential look, but, to my unspeakable confusion, found her back turned upon me.

' I had now nothing left for it but to make
amends for all by handing her to her chair. I
bustled through the crowd, and got to her
box-door as soon as possible, when, to my
utter confusion, the young puppy, I have been
telling you of before, bolted out upon me with
Mrs. Lucy in his hand. I could not have
started back with greater precipitation if I
had met a ghost. The malicious gipsy took
no notice of me, but turning aside her head
said something to her dog of a gentleman-
usher, with a smile that went to my heart. I
could not sleep all night for it, and the next
morning writ the following letter to her.

' " Madam,—I protest I mean nothing by
what passed last night, and beg you will put
the most candid interpretation upon my looks
and actions ; for however my eyes may wander, there is none but Mrs. Lucy who has the
entire possession of my heart.—I am, Madam,
with a passion that is not to be expressed
either by looks, words, or actions, your most
unalienable, and most humble Servant,

" Tom Whiffle."

' And now, Sir, what do you think was her

answer? Why, to give you a true notion of her, and that you may guess at all her cursed tricks by this one—Here it is.

'" Mr. Whiffle,—I am very much surprised to hear you talk of anything that passed between us last night, when to the best of my remembrance I have not seen you these three days. Your Servant,   L. T."'

No. 9.—Tuesday, March 16

'Quantâ laboras in Charybdi!'—Hor.

Upon my opening the lovers' box this morning, I found nothing in it but the following letter, made up very nicely, and sealed with a little cupid holding a flaming heart in each hand, and circumscribed 'Love unites us.' I find, by the contents of this letter, that my correspondent will soon change his device, and perhaps make the figure of Hymen perform that part which, at present, he has assigned to Cupid.

'Sir,—As you are a man of experience in the world, I beg your advice in a matter of great importance to me. I have, for some time, been engaged in close friendship with a fine woman: your knowledge of mankind will easily inform you of the purport of that phrase. In short, I have lived with her, as with a she-friend, in the utmost propriety of

221

that term ; but, at present, I am under a very
great embarrass ; for having run out most of
my fortune, in the course of my conversation
with her, I find myself necessitated to go into
a new way of life, and by that means to make
myself whole again. A favourable opportunity presents itself: a rich widow (the
common refuge of us idle fellows) has spoke
kindly of me, and I have reason to believe
will very shortly put me in possession of her
person and jointure. Tell me, dear Mr. Myrtle,
how I shall communicate this affair to the
poor creature whom I am going to forsake.
If I know her temper, she loves me so well
that she would rather see me beggared and
undone, than in a state of wealth and ease
with another woman. She will call my en-
deavours to make myself happy, being false
to her. Nay, I don't know but she may be
fool enough to make away with herself; for
the last time I talked to her, and mentioned
this affair at a distance, she seemed to show a
cursed hankering after purling streams. Let
me conjure thee, old Marmaduke, if thou wilt
not give me some advice, to give some to this
poor woman; make her sensible that a man
does not take a mistress for better for worse,
and that there is some difference between a
lover and a husband ; but you know better
than I can tell you, what to say upon so nice
a subject.—I am, your most humble Servant,
‘ W. T.’

There is nothing which I more abhor, than that kind of wit which betrays a hardness of heart. Inhumanity is never so odious, as when it is practised with mirth and wantonness. If I may make so free with my correspondent, he seems to be a man of this unlucky turn. I shall not fall into the same fault which I condemn in him; but, that I may be serious on such an occasion, will desire my readers to consider throughly the evils which they are heaping up to themselves, when they engage in a criminal amour. If they die in it, they know very well what must be the dreadful consequence. If either of them break loose from the other, the melancholy and vexation that are produced on such occasions, are too dear a payment for those pleasures which preceded, and are past, as though they had never been.

The woman is generally the greatest sufferer in cases of this nature; for by the long observations I have made on both sexes, I have established this as a maxim, that 'women dissemble their passions better than men, but that men subdue their passions better than women.

I have heard a story to my present purpose, which has very much affected me. The gentleman from whom I heard it was an eyewitness of several parts of it.

About ten years ago there lived at Vienna a German count, who had long entertained a

223

secret amour with a young lady of a considerable family. After a correspondence of gallantries, which had lasted two or three years, the father of the young count, whose family was reduced to a low condition, found out a very advantageous match for him, and made his son sensible that he ought, in common prudence, to close with it. The count, upon the first opportunity, acquainted his mistress very fairly with what had passed, and laid the whole matter before her, with such freedom and openness of heart, that she seemingly consented to it. She only desired of him that they might have one meeting more, before they parted for ever. The place appointed for this their meeting, was a grove which stands at a little distance from the town. They conversed together in this place for some time, when on a sudden the lady pulled out a pocket-pistol, and shot her lover into the heart, so that he immediately fell down dead at her feet. She then returned to her father's house, telling every one she met what she had done. Her friends, upon hearing her story, would have found out means for her to make her escape; but she told them she had killed her dear count, because she could not live without him; and that for the same reason she was resolved to follow him by whatever way justice should determine. She was no sooner seized, but she avowed her guilt, rejected all excuses that were made in her favour, and only begged that her execution might be speedy. She was sentenced to have her head cut off, and was apprehensive of nothing but that the interest of her friends should obtain a pardon for her. When the confessor approached her, she asked him where he thought was the soul of the dead count? He replied, that his case was very dangerous, considering the circumstances in which he died. Upon this so desperate was her frenzy, that she bid him leave her, for that she was resolved to go to the same place where the count was. The priest was forced to give her better hopes of the deceased, from considerations that he was upon the point of breaking off so criminal a commerce, and leading a new life, before he could bring her mind to a temper fit for one who was so near her end. Upon the day of her execution she dressed herself in all her ornaments, and walked towards the scaffold more like an expecting bride than a condemned criminal. My friend tells me, that he saw her placed in the chair, according to the custom of that place, where after having stretched out her neck with an air of joy, she called upon the name of the count, which was the appointed signal for the executioner, who, with a single blow of his sword, severed her head from her body.

My reader may draw, without my assistance, a suitable moral out of so tragical a story.

No. 11.—Saturday, March 20.

Mæcenas Atavis edite regibus.
Bentley's ' Horace.'

The following epistle is written to me from
the parish of Gotham in Herefordshire, from
one who had credentials from me to be received as an humble servant to a young lady
of the family which he mentions; because it
may be an instruction to all who court great
alliances, I shall insert it word for word as it
came to my hands.

'Sweet Mr. Myrtle,—According to your
persuasion I came down here into the country,
with a design to ingraft myself into the family
to which you recommended me ; but I wish
you had thought a little more of it before you
gave me that advice, for a man is not always
made happy by having settled himself in a
powerful house ; for riches and honour are
ornamental to the possessors of 'em only
when those possessors have such arts or
endowments which would render them conspicuous without them ; but these creatures
to whom you advised me to be allied are
such, whose interest it is to court privacy,
and are made up of so many defects, that
they could not better recommend themselves
to the world, or consult their own interest,
than by hiding ; but they are so little inclined

to such a prudent behaviour, that they seem
to think that their appearance upon all occasions cannot choose but be advantageous to
them; and yet such is the force of nature in
biassing all its instruments to the uses for
which she has made them most fit, that they
are ever undertaking what would make the
most beautiful of human race appear as ugly
as themselves. Thus they take upon them
to manage all things in this country; and if
any man is to be accused, arrested, or dis-
graced, one of these hideous creatures has
certainly a hand in it. By these methods and
arts they govern those who contemn them,
and are perpetually followed by crowds who
hate them: at the same time there is I know
not what excessively comic and diverting to
behold these very odd fellows in their magni-
ficencies.

'You must know they set up extremely for
genealogies, old codes, and mystic writings,
and knowing abundance of what was never
worth knowing in the several ages in which
it was acted; but there is constantly, in all
they pretend to, some circumstance which
secretly tends to raise the honour and antiquity of their family. Thus they are not contented, as all we the rest of the world are,
to become more ancient every day than other
as time passes on, but they grow old backwards, and every now and then they make
some new purchase of musty rolls and papers,

which they tell you acquaints them with some new matter concerning their further antiquity. I met here, to my great surprise, Abednego the Jew, who used to transfer stock for me at Change-Ally. I was going to salute him, but he tipped me the wink, and taking me apart at a proper opportunity, desired me not to discover him, For, says he, laughing, I am come down here as a cheat; he explained himself further, that his way was to get some paper that was mouldy, dusty, or moth-eaten, and write upon it Hebrew characters, which he sold to Sir Anthony Crab-tree's Library; you must know there is nothing so monstrous but they can make pass upon the people; so terrible are the Crab-trees in this county. The last piece of antiquity which they produced, was a letter written in Noah's own hand to their ancestor, and found upon a mountain in Wales (which, by the way, is said by them to be the oldest and highest mountain in the world), directed to their ancestor, Sir Robert Crab-tree, an antediluvian knight. This, sir, passes very currently here, and is well received, because all allow there have been no faces like theirs in any other family since the Flood.

'It would be endless to give you a distinct account of these worthies in one letter, but I will go as far as I can in it. I was, when I declared my love, appointed an hour in their great hall, where were assembled all their

relations and tenants; but instead of receiving
me with civility, as one who desired to be of
their family, as they know not how to show
power and greatness, but by doing things
terrible and disagreeable, Mr. Peter Brickdust stands up before all the company, and
enters into a downright invective against
me, to show that I was not fit to be entertained among them. They call him here, at
Gotham and in all these parts, the Accuser,
because it is his natural propensity to think
the worst of every man. Tho' the implement
has a very great estate, the poverty of his
soul is such, that he will do anything for a
further penny. He condescends to audit part
of the rents of Sir Anthony's estate, and, tho'
born to a better fortune than the Knight himself, is his utter slave. His business about
him is to find out somebody or other for him,
from time to time, on whom to exercise his
great power and interest. Peter has the very
look of a wicked one of low practice. Peter
is made for a lurcher, and as being a creature
of prey, he rises to the object he aims at, as
if he were going to spring at some game;
but he slinks, as you may have seen a cur
at once exert and check his little anger when
he sees a strange mastiff. Naturalists say
all men have something in their aspect of
other animals, which resemble them in constitution. Peter's countenance discovers him a
creature of small prey, it is a mixture of the face

RICHARD STEELE

of a cat, and that of an owl. He has the spiteful
eagerness of the former, blended with the
stupid gravity of the latter. He stood behind
a post all the while he was talking, and groped
it as if he were feeling for hobnails. All that
he said was so extravagant, wild, and groundless, and urged with a mien so suitable to the
falsehood and folly of it, that I was rather
diverted than offended at Brickdust. When
from another quarter of the hall, placed just
under a gallery, there stood up the Knight's
brother. It is impossible to express the par-
ticularity of this gentleman. His mien is like
that of a broken tradesman the first day he
wears a sword; his aspect was sad, but
rather the face of a man incapable of mirth,
than under any sorrow, and yet he does not
look dull neither, but attentive to both worlds
at once, and has in his brow both the usurer
and the saint. I observed great respect paid
to him; but methought some leavings of conscience made him look somewhat abashed
at the great civilities which were paid him.
He roundly asserted I was not worth a groat,
and indeed made it out in a moment; for, by
some trick or other, he had got in his custody
all the writings which make out the title to
my estate.

'What made this whole matter the more
extravagantly pleasant was, that there is an
odd droning loudness in the brother's voice,
which made a large Irish greyhound open at

every pause he made. That great surly
creature made so docile and servile, was to
me matter of much entertainment and curiosity. The Knight's brother, I assure you,
spoke with a good steady impudence, and
having been long inured to talk what he does
not mean, he looks as if he meant what he
said.

'The pleasantry of this excellent farce is,
that all these fellows were bred Presbyterians,
and are now set up for High Churchmen.
They carry it admirably well, and the par-
tisans do not distinguish that there is a difference between those who are of neither side,
from generous principles, and those who are
disinterested only from having no principles
at all. The Knight himself was not in the
country, but is expected every day; they say
he is a precious one. They make me expect
he will treat me after another way. His
manner is very droll; he is very affable, and
yet keeps you at a distance; for he talks to
everybody, but will let nobody understand
him. Here is a gentleman in the country, a
good intelligent companion, that gives me a
very pleasant idea of him; he says he has
seen him go through his great hall full of
company, and whisper every man as he
passed along; when they have all had the
whisper, they have held up their heads in a
silly amazement, like geese when they are
drinking. But perhaps more of this another

time; you would marry me into this goodly
house.—I thank you for nothing, dear sir, and
am your humble servant for that.

'P.S.—Here is a story here that Mr. What
d'e-call laughs at all they pretend to do
against him, and is prepared for the worst
that can happen. To inure himself to be a
public spectacle, they say, he rid an hour
and a half at noon-day on Wednesday last,
behind Charles the First at Charing Cross.'

ALEXANDER SELKIRK

('The Englishman,' No. 26.)

Under the title of this paper, I do not think
it foreign to my design, to speak of a man
born in Her Majesty's dominions, and relate
an adventure in his life so uncommon, that
it's doubtful whether the like has happened
to any other of human race. The person I
speak of, is Alexander Selkirk, whose name
is familiar to men of curiosity, from the fame
of his having lived four years and four months
alone in the island of Juan Fernandez. I had
the pleasure frequently to converse with the
man soon after his arrival in England, in the
year 1711. It was matter of great curiosity
to hear him, as he is a man of good sense,
give an account of the different revolutions in
his own mind in that long solitude. When
we consider how painful absence from com-

pany, for the space of but one evening, is to the generality of mankind, we may have a sense how painful this necessary and constant solitude was to a man bred a sailor, and ever accustomed to enjoy, and suffer, eat, drink, and sleep, and perform all offices of life in fellowship and company. He was put ashore from a leaky vessel, with the captain of which he had had an irreconcilable difference; and he chose rather to take his fate in this place, than in a crazy vessel, under a disagreeable commander. His portion were a sea-chest, his wearing clothes and bedding, a fire-lock, a pound of gunpowder, a large quantity of bullets, a flint and steel, a few pounds of tobacco, an hatchet, a knife, a kettle, a Bible, and other books of devotion; together with pieces that concerned navigation, and his mathematical instruments. Resentment against his officer, who had ill-used him, made him look forward to this change of life as the more eligible one, till the instant in which he saw the vessel put off, at which moment his heart yearned within him, and melted at the parting with his comrades and all human society at once. He had in provisions for the sustenance of life, but the quantity of two meals, the island abounding only with wild goats, cats, and rats. He judged it most probable, that he should find more immediate and easy relief, by finding shell-fish on the shore, than seeking game

233

with his gun. He accordingly found great quantities of turtles, whose flesh is extremely delicious, and of which he frequently ate very plentifully on his first arrival, till it grew disagreeable to his stomach, except in jellies. The necessities of hunger and thirst were his greatest diversions from the reflection on his lonely condition. When those appetites were satisfied, the desire of society was as strong a call upon him, and he appeared to himself least necessitous when he wanted everything; for the supports of his body were easily attained, but the eager longings for seeing again the face of man, during the interval of craving bodily appetites, were hardly supportable. He grew dejected, languid, and melancholy, scarce able to restrain from doing himself violence, till by degrees, by the force of reason, and frequent reading of the Scriptures, and turning his thoughts upon the study of navigation, after the space of eighteen months, he grew thoroughly reconciled to his condition. When he had made this conquest, the vigour of his health, disengagement from the world, a constant, cheerful, serene sky, and a temperate air, made his life one continual feast, and his being much more joyful than it had before been irksome. He now taking delight in everything, made the hut, in which he lay, by ornaments which he cut down from a spacious wood, on the side of which it was situated, the most delicious

234

bower, fanned with continual breezes and
gentle aspirations of wind, that made his
repose after the chase equal to the most
sensual pleasures.

I forget to observe, that during the time
of his dissatisfaction, monsters of the deep,
which frequently lay on the shore, added to
the terrors of his solitude, the dreadful howl-
ings and voices seemed too terrible to be
made for human ears; but upon the recovery
of his temper, he could with pleasure not only
hear their voices, but approach the monsters
themselves with great intrepidity. He speaks
of sea-lions, whose jaws and tails were
capable of seizing or breaking the limbs of
a man, if he approached them: but at that
time his spirits and life were so high, that he
could act so regularly and unconcerned, that
merely from being unruffled in himself, he
killed them with the greatest ease imaginable: for observing that tho' their jaws
and tails were so terrible, yet the animals
being mighty slow in working themselves
round, he had nothing to do but place himself
exactly opposite to their middle, and as close
to them as possible, and he dispatched them
with his hatchet at will.

The precautions which he took against
want, in case of sickness, was to lame kids
when very young, so as that they might
recover their health, but never be capable of
speed. These he had in great numbers about

his hut; and when he was himself in full vigour, he could take at full speed the swiftest goat running up a promontory, and never failed of catching them, but on a descent.

His habitation was extremely pestered with rats, which gnawed his clothes and feet when sleeping. To defend him against them, he fed and tamed numbers of young kitlings, who lay about his bed, and preserved him from the enemy. When his clothes were quite worn out, he dried and tacked together the skins of goats, with which he clothed himself, and was enured to pass through woods, bushes, and brambles with as much carelessness and precipitance as any other animal. It happened once to him, that running on the summit of a hill, he made a stretch to seize a goat; with which under him, he fell down a precipice, and lay senseless for the space of three days, the length of which time he measured by the moon's growth since his last observation. This manner of life grew so exquisitely pleasant, that he never had a moment heavy upon his hands; his nights were untroubled, and his days joyous, from the practice of temperance and exercise. It was his manner to use stated hours and places for exercises of devotion, which he performed aloud, in order to keep up the faculties of speech, and to utter himself with greater energy.

When I first saw him, I thought, if I had

RICHARD STEELE

not been let into his character and story, I
could have discerned that he had been much
separated from company, from his aspect and
gesture; there was a strong but cheerful
seriousness in his look, and a certain dis-
regard to the ordinary things about him, as
if he had been sunk in thought. When the
ship, which brought him off the island, came
in, he received them with the greatest indifference, with relation to the prospect of going
off with them, but with great satisfaction in
an opportunity to refresh and help them; the
man frequently bewailed his return to the
world, which could not, he said, with all its
enjoyments, restore him to the tranquillity
of his solitude. Tho' I had frequently conversed with him, after a few months' absence,
he met me in the street; and though he spoke
to me, I could not recollect that I had seen
him : familiar converse in this town had taken
off the loneliness of his aspect, and quite
altered the air of his face.

This plain man's story is a memorable
example, that he is happiest who confines
his wants to natural necessities ; and he that
goes further in his desires, increases his
wants in proportion to his acquisitions; or to
use his own expression, 'I am now worth
eight hundred pounds, but shall never be so
happy as when I was not worth a farthing.'

RICHARD STEELE

('Tatler,' No. 95.)

There are several persons who have many
pleasures and entertainments in their possession which they do not enjoy. It is therefore
a kind and good office to acquaint them with
their own happiness, and turn their attention
to such instances of their good fortune which
they are apt to overlook. Persons in the
married state often want such a monitor, and
pine away their days, by looking upon the
same condition in anguish and murmur,
which carries with it in the opinion of others
a complication of all the pleasures of life, and
a retreat from its inquietudes.

I am led into this thought by a visit I made
an old friend, who was formerly my school-
fellow. He came to town last week with his
family for the winter, and yesterday morning
sent me word his wife expected me to dinner.
I am as it were at home at that house, and
every member of it knows me for their well-
wisher. I cannot indeed express the pleasure
it is, to be met by the children with so much
joy as I am when I go thither. The boys and
girls strive who shall come first, when they
think it is I that am knocking at the door;
and that child which loses the race to me,
runs back again to tell the father it is Mr.
Bickerstaff. This day I was led in by a pretty
238

girl, that we all thought must have forgot me; for the family has been out of town these two years. Her knowing me again was a mighty subject with us, and took up our discourse at the first entrance. After which they began to rally me upon a thousand little stories they heard in the country, about my marriage to one of my neighbour's daughters. Upon which the gentleman my friend said, Nay, if Mr. Bickerstaff marries a child of any of his old companions, I hope mine shall have the preference; there's Mrs. Mary is now sixteen, and would make him as fine a widow as the best of them. But I know him too well; he is so enamoured with the very memory of those who flourished in our youth, that he will not so much as look upon the modern beauties. I remember, old gentleman, how often you went home in a day to refresh your countenance and dress, when Teraminta reigned in your heart. As we came up in the coach, I repeated to my wife some of your verses on her. With such reflections on little passages which happened long ago, we passed our time during a cheerful and elegant meal. After dinner, his lady left the room, as did also the children. As soon as we were alone, he took me by the hand: Well, my good friend, says he, I am heartily glad to see thee; I was afraid you would never have seen all the company that dined with you to-day again. Do not you

think the good woman of the house a little
altered, since you followed her from the play-
house, to find out who she was, for me? I
perceived a tear fall down his cheek as he
spoke, which moved me not a little. But to
turn the discourse, said I, She is not indeed
quite that creature she was when she returned me the letter I carried from you; and
told me, She hoped, as I was a gentleman,
I would be employ'd no more to trouble her
who had never offended me, but would be so
much the gentleman's friend as to dissuade
him from a pursuit which he could never
succeed in. You may remember, I thought
her in earnest, and you were forced to employ your cousin Will, who made his sister
get acquainted with her for you. You cannot
expect her to be for ever fifteen. Fifteen?
replied my good friend: Ah! You little
understand, you that have lived a bachelor,
how great, how exquisite, a pleasure there is
in being really beloved! It is impossible that
the most beauteous face in nature should raise
in me such pleasing ideas, as when I look
upon that excellent woman. That fading in
her countenance is chiefly caused by her
watching me in my fever. This was followed
by a fit of sickness, which had like to have
carried her off last winter. I tell you sincerely,
I have so many obligations to her, that I
cannot with any sort of moderation think of
her present state of health. But as to what

240

you say of fifteen, she gives me every day
pleasures beyond what I ever knew in the
possession of her beauty, when I was in the
vigour of youth. Every moment of her life
brings me fresh instances of her complacency
to my inclinations, and her prudence in regard
to my fortune. Her face is to me much more
beautiful than when I first saw it ; there is no
decay in any feature which I cannot trace
from the very instant it was occasioned, by
some anxious concern for my welfare and
interests. Thus at the same time, methinks,
the love I conceived towards her for what she
was, is heightened by my gratitude for what
she is. The love of a wife is as much above
the idle passion commonly called by that
name, as the loud laughter of buffoons is
inferior to the elegant mirth of gentlemen.
Oh! she is an inestimable jewel. In her
examination of her household affairs, she
shows a certain fearfulness to find a fault,
which makes her servants obey her like
children ; and the meanest we have, has an
ingenuous shame for an offence, not always
to be seen in children in other families. I
speak freely to you, my old friend, ever since
her sickness, things that gave me the quickest
joy before, turn now to a certain anxiety.
As the children play in the next room, I know
the poor things by their steps, and am considering what they must do, should they lose
their mother in their tender years. The plea-

sure I used to take in telling my boy stories
of battles, and asking my girl questions about
the disposal of her baby, and the gossiping
of it, is turned into inward reflection and
melancholy.

He would have gone on in this tender way,
when the good lady entered, and, with an
inexpressible sweetness in her countenance,
told us, she had been searching her closet for
something very good, to treat such an old
friend as I was. Her husband's eyes sparkled
with pleasure at the cheerfulness of her
countenance; and I saw all his fears vanish
in an instant. The lady observing something in our looks which showed we had
been more serious than ordinary, and seeing
her husband receive her with great concern
under a forced cheerfulness, immediately
guessed at what we had been talking of;
and, applying herself to me, said, with a
smile, Mr. Bickerstaff, do not believe a
word of what he tells you: I shall still live
to have you for my second, as I have often
promised you, unless he takes more care of
himself than he has done since his coming to
town. You must know, he tells me, That he
finds London is a much more healthy place
than the country; for he sees several of his
old acquaintance and schoolfellows are here,
young fellows with full-bottomed periwigs.
I could scarce keep him this morning from
going out open-breasted. My friend, who

is always extremely delighted with her agreeable humour, made her sit down with us.
She did it with that easiness which is peculiar
to women of sense ; and to keep up the good
humour she had brought in with her, turned
her raillery upon me. Mr. Bickerstaff, you
remember you followed me one night from
the playhouse ; supposing you should carry
me thither to-morrow night, and lead me into
the front box. This put us into a long field
of discourse about the beauties, who were
mothers to the present, and shined in the
boxes twenty years ago. I told her, I was
glad she had transferred so many of her
charms, and I did not question but her eldest
daughter was within half a year of being a
toast.

We were pleasing ourselves with this
fantastical preferment of the young lady,
when on a sudden we were alarmed with the
noise of a drum, and immediately entered my
little godson to give me a point of war. His
mother, between laughing and chiding, would
have put him out of the room ; but I would
not part with him so. I found, upon conversation with him, though he was a little noisy in
his mirth, that the child had excellent parts,
and was a great master of all the learning
on t'other side eight years old. I perceived
him a very great historian in ' Æsop's Fables,'
but he frankly declared to me his mind, That
he did not delight in that learning, because he

did not believe they were true; for which
reason, I found he had very much turned his
studies for about a twelvemonth past, into
the lives and adventures of Don Bellianis of
Greece, Guy of Warwick, the Seven Champions, and other historians of that age. I
could not but observe the satisfaction the father
took in the forwardness of his son; and that
these diversions might turn to some profit, I
found the boy had made remarks, which
might be of service to him during the course
of his whole life. He would tell you the
mismanagements of John Hickathrift, find
fault with the passionate temper in Bevis of
Southampton, and love St. George for being
the champion of England; and by this means,
had his thoughts insensibly moulded into the
notions of discretion, virtue, and honour. I
was extolling his accomplishments, when the
mother told me, That the little girl who led
me in this morning, was in her way a better
scholar than he. Betty (says she) deals chiefly
in fairies and sprites; and sometimes in a
winter night, will terrify the maids with her
accounts, till they are afraid to go up to
bed.

I sat with them till it was very late, sometimes in merry, sometimes in serious discourse,
with this particular pleasure, which gives the
only true relish to all conversation, a sense
that every one of us liked each other. I went
home, considering the different conditions of

a married life and that of a bachelor; and I must confess, it struck me with a secret concern, to reflect, that whenever I go off, I shall leave no traces behind me. In this pensive mood I returned to my family; that is to say, to my maid, my dog and my cat, who can only be the better or worse for what happens to me.

BISHOP BERKELEY

(From the 'Guardian')

'Multa putans sortemque animo miseratus
    iniquam.'   Virg. 'Ænid' 6, v. 332.
Struck with compassion of so sad a state.

In compassion to those gloomy mortals
who by their unbelief are rendered incapable
of feeling those impressions of joy and hope
which the celebration of the late glorious
festival naturally leaves on the mind of a
Christian, I shall in this paper endeavour to
evince that there are grounds to expect a
Future State without supposing in the reader
any faith at all, not even the belief of a Deity.
Let the most steadfast unbeliever open his
eyes and take a survey of the sensible world,
and then say if there be not a connection, an
adjustment, an exact and constant order dis-
coverable in all the parts of it. Whatever be
the cause, the thing itself is evident to all our
faculties. Look into the animal system—the
passions, senses, and locomotive powers, is
not the like contrivance and propriety observable in these too? Are they not fitted to
certain ends, and are they not by nature
directed to proper objects?

Is it possible, then, that the smallest bodies should, by a management superior to the wit of man, be disposed in the most excellent manner agreeable to their respective natures, and yet the spirits or souls of men be neglected or managed by such rules as fall short of man's understanding?

Shall every other passion be rightly placed by nature and shall that appetite of Immortality natural to all mankind be alone misplaced or designed to be frustrated? Shall the industrious application of the inferior animal powers in the meanest vocations be answered by the ends we propose and shall not the generous efforts of a virtuous mind be rewarded? In a word, shall the corporeal world be all order and harmony, the intellectual disorder and confusion? He who is bigot enough to believe these things must bid adieu to that natural rule of 'reasoning from analogy,' must run counter to that maxim of common sense, 'that men ought to form their judgment of things unexperienced from what they have experienced.'

If anything looks like a recompense of calamitous virtue on this side the grave it is either an assurance that thereby we obtain the favour and protection of Heaven, and shall, whatever befalls us in this, in another life meet with a just return, or else that applause and reputation which is thought to attend virtuous actions. The former of these our

Free-thinkers, out of their singular wisdom and
benevolence to mankind, endeavour to erase
from the minds of men. The latter can never
be justly distributed in this life where so many
ill actions are reputable and so many good
actions disesteemed or misinterpreted, where
subtle hypocrisy is placed in the most engaging light and modest virtue lies concealed,
where the heart and the soul are hid from the
eyes of men, and the eyes of men are dimmed
and vitiated. Plato's sense was contained in
his Gorgias, where he introduces Socrates
speaking after this manner: 'It was in the
reign of Saturn provided by a law which the
gods have since continued down to this time,
that they who had lived virtuously and piously
upon earth should after death enjoy a life
full of happiness in certain islands appointed
for the habitation of the blessed ; but that
such as have lived wickedly should go into
the receptacle of damned souls named Tartarus, there to suffer the punishments they
deserved. But in all the reign of Saturn and
in the beginning of the reign of Jove, living
judges were appointed by whom each person
was judged in his lifetime in the same day on
which he was to die. The consequence of
which was that they often passed wrong
judgments. Pluto, therefore, who presided
in Tartarus, and the guardians of the blessed
islands, finding that on the other side many
unfit persons were sent to their respective

dominions, complained to Jove, who promised
to redress the evil. He added, the reasons of
these unjust proceedings are that men are
judged in the body. Hence many conceal
the blemishes and imperfections of their minds
by beauty, birth, and riches, not to mention
that at the time of trial there are crowds of
witnesses to attest their having lived well.
These things mislead the judges, who being
themselves also of the number of the living,
are surrounded each with his own body as
with a veil thrown over his mind. For the
future, therefore, it is my intention that men
do not come on their trial till after death,
when they shall appear before the judge dis-
robed of all their corporeal ornaments. The
judge himself, too, shall be a pure, unveiled
spirit, beholding the very soul, the naked soul,
of the party before him.

'With this view I have already constituted
my sons, Minos and Rhadamanthus, judges,
who are natives of Asia, and Æachus, a native
of Europe. These, after death, shall hold
their court in a certain meadow from which
there are two roads leading, the one to
Tartarus, the other to the islands of "the
blessed."'

From this, as from numberless other passages of his writings, may be seen Plato's
opinion of a Future State. A thing, therefore,
in regard to us so comfortable in itself, so
just and excellent a thing, so agreeable to

the analogy of nature, and so universally credited by all orders and ranks of men of all nations and ages, what is it that should move a few men to reject? Surely there must be something of prejudice in the case. I appeal to the secret thoughts of a Free-thinker if he does not argue within himself after this manner: The senses and faculties I enjoy at present are visibly designed to repair or preserve the body from the injuries it is liable to in its present circumstances; but in an eternal state where no decays are to be repaired, no outward injuries to be fenced against, where there are no flesh and bones, nerves or blood-vessels, there will certainly be none of the senses, and that there should be a state of life without the senses is inconceivable.

But as this manner of reasoning proceeds from a poverty of imagination and narrowness of soul in those that use it, I shall endeavour to remedy those defects and open their views, by laying before them a case which, being naturally possible, may perhaps reconcile them to the belief of what is supernaturally revealed.

Let us suppose a person blind and deaf from his birth who, being grown to man's estate, is by the dead palsy or some other cause, deprived of his feeling, tasting, and smelling, and at the same time has the impediment of his hearing removed and the film

taken from his eyes. What the five senses
are to us that the touch, taste, and smell
were to him. And any other ways of perception of a more refined and extensive nature
were to him as inconceivable, as to us those
are which will one day be adapted to perceive
those things which 'eye hath not seen nor
ear heard, neither hath it entered into the
heart of man to conceive.' And it would be
just as reasonable in him to conclude that the
loss of those three senses could not possibly
be succeeded by any new inlets of perception,
as in a modern Free-thinker to imagine there
can be no state of life and perception without
the senses he enjoys at present. Let us
further suppose the same person's eyes, at
their first opening, to be struck with a great
variety of the most gay and pleasing objects,
and his ears with a melodious consort of vocal
and instrumental music. Behold him amazed,
ravished, transported! and you have some
distant representation, some faint and glim-
mering idea of the ecstatic state of the soul
in that article in which she emerges from this
sepulchre of flesh into Life and Immortality.

'O vitæ philosophia dux virtutis indagatrix.'
                                        Cicero.
O philosophy, thou guide of life, and discoverer
of virtue.

To Nestor Ironside, Esq.

'Sir,—I am a man who have spent great
part of that time in rambling through foreign
countries which young gentlemen usually
pass at the university, by which course of life,
although I have acquired no small insight
into the manners and conversation of men,
yet I could not make proportionable advances
in the way of science and speculation.

'In my return through France, as I was
one day setting forth this my case to a certain
gentleman of that nation with whom I had
contracted a friendship; after some pause he
conducted me into his closet, and opening a
little amber cabinet, took from thence a small
box of snuff, which he said was given him
by an uncle of his, the author of " The Voyage
to the World of Descartes," and with many
professions of gratitude and friendship made
me a present of it, telling me at the same time
that he knew no readier way to furnish and
adorn a mind with knowledge in the arts and
sciences than that same snuff rightly applied.

'You must know, said he, that Descartes
was the first who discovered a certain part
of the brain called by anatomists the pineal

gland to be the immediate receptacle of the soul, where she is affected with all sorts of perceptions, and exerts all her operations by the intercourse of the animal spirits which run through the nerves that are thence extended to all parts of the body. He added, that the same philosopher having considered the body as a machine or piece of clockwork, which performed all the vital operations without the concurrence of the will, began to think a way may be found out for separating the soul for some time from the body without any injury to the latter, and that after much meditation on that subject, the above-mentioned virtuoso composed the snuff he then gave me, which, if taken in a certain quantity, would not fail to disengage my soul from my body. Your soul (continued he) being at liberty to transport herself with a thought wherever she pleases, may enter into the pineal gland of the most learned philosopher, and being so placed, become spectator of all the ideas in his mind, which would instruct her in much less time than the usual methods.

'I returned him thanks and accepted his present, and with it a paper of directions.

'You may imagine it was no small improvement and diversion to pass my time in the pineal glands of philosophers, poets, beaux, mathematicians, ladies, and statesmen. One while to trace a theorem in mathematics through a long labyrinth of intricate turns

253

and subtleties of thought; another to be conscious of the sublime ideas and comprehensive views of a philosopher, without any fatigue or wasting of my own spirits.

'Sometimes to wander through perfumed groves or enamelled meadows in the fancy of a poet; at others to be present when a battle or storm raged, or a glittering palace rose in his imagination, or to behold the pleasures of a country life, the passion of a generous love, or the warmth of devotion wrought up to rapture.

'Or (to use the words of a very ingenious author) to

Behold the raptures which a writer knows
When in his breast a vein of fancy glows,
Behold his business while he works the
    mine,
Behold his temper when he sees it shine.

'These gave me inconceivable pleasure. Nor was it an unpleasant entertainment sometimes to descend from these sublime and magnificent ideas to the impertinences of a beau, the dry schemes of a coffee-house politician or the tender images in the mind of a young lady.

'And as in order to frame a right idea of human happiness I thought it expedient to make a trial of the various manners wherein men of different pursuits were affected, I one day entered into the pineal gland of a certain person who seemed very fit to give me an insight into all that which constitutes the happiness of him who is called "a man of pleasure."

'But I found myself not a little disappointed in my notion of the pleasures which attend a voluptuary who has shaken off the restraints of reason.

'His intellectuals, I observed, were grown unserviceable by too little use, and his senses were decayed and worn out by too much. That perfect inaction of the higher powers prevented appetite in prompting him to sensual gratifications, and the outrunning natural appetite produced a loathing instead of a pleasure. I there beheld the intemperate cravings of youth without the enjoyments of it, and the weakness of old age without its tranquillity. When the passions were teazed and roused by some powerful object, the effect was not to delight or soothe the mind but to torture it between the returning extremes of appetite and satiety.

'I saw a wretch racked at the same time with a painful remembrance of past mis-carriages, a distaste of the present objects that solicit his senses and a secret dread of futurity. And I could see no manner of relief or comfort in the soul of this miserable man but what consisted in preventing his cure by inflaming his passions and suppressing his reason.

255

' But though it must be owned he had almost quenched that light which his Creator had set up in his soul, yet in spite of all his efforts I observed at certain seasons frequent flashes of remorse strike through the gloom and interrupt that satisfaction he enjoyed in hiding his own deformities from himself.

' I was also present at the original formation or production of a certain book in the mind of a Free-thinker, and believing it may be not inacceptable to let you into the secret manner, and now and then carry him to church, by which means he may in time come to a right sense of religion and wear off the ill impressions he has received. Lastly, I would advise whoever undertakes the reformation of a modern Free-thinker that above all things he be careful to subdue his vanity, that being the principal motive which prompts a little genius to distinguish itself by singularities that are hurtful to mankind.

' Or if the passion of vanity, as it is for the most part very strong in your Free-thinkers, cannot be subdued, let it be won over to the interest of religion by giving them to understand that the greatest genii of the age have a respect for things sacred, that their rhapsodies find no admirers and that the name Free-thinker, like tyrant of old, degenerated from its original signification, and is now supposed to denote something contrary to wit and reason. In fine, let them know that whatever temptations a few men of parts might formerly have had from the novelty of the thing to oppose the received opinions of Christians, yet that now the humour is worn out and blasphemy and irreligion are distinctions which have long since descended down to lackeys and drawers.

'But it must be my business to prevent all pretenders in this kind from hurting the ignorant and unwary. In order to this, I communicated an intelligence which I received of a gentleman's appearing very sorry that he was not well during a late fit of sickness, contrary to his own doctrine, which obliged him to be merry on that occasion, except he was sure of recovering. Upon this advice to the world, the following advertisement got a place in the "Postboy."

'"Whereas in the paper called the 'Guardian' of Saturday the 11th inst., a corollary reflection was made on Monsieur D—— a member of the Royal Academy of Sciences in Paris, author of a book lately published, entitled: 'A Philosophical Essay, or Reflections on the death of Free-thinkers, with the characters of the most eminent persons of both sexes, ancient and modern, that died pleasantly and unconcerned,' etc.; sold by I. Baker in Paternoster Row—suggesting as if that gentleman now in London,

was very much out of humour in a late fit
of sickness till he was in a fair way of
recovery: this is to assure the public that the
said gentleman never expressed the least
concern at the approach of death, but
expected the fatal minute with a most
heroical and philosophical resignation, of
which a copy of verses he wrote in the
serene intervals of his distemper is an invincible proof."

'All that I contend for is, that this gentleman was out of humour when he was sick,
and the advertiser to confute me says that
in the serene intervals of his distemper, that
is when he was not sick, he wrote verses.

'I shall not retract my advertisement till
I see those verses, and I will choose what
to believe then except they are underwritten
by his nurse, nor then neither except she is
an house-keeper. I must tie this gentleman
close to the argument, for if he had not
actually his fit upon him there is nothing
courageous in the thing, nor does it make
for his purpose, nor are they heroic verses.

'The point of being merry at the hour of
death is a matter that ought to be settled
by divines, but the publisher of the " Philological Essay" produces his chief authorities
from Lucretius, the Earl of Rochester, and
Mr. John Dryden, who were gentlemen that
did not think themselves obliged to prove all

they said, or else proved their assertions by
saying or swearing they were all fools who
believed to the contrary. If it be absolutely
necessary that a man should be facetious at
his death, it would be very well if these
gentlemen, Monsieur D—— and Mr. B——
would repent betimes and not trust to a
death-bed ingenuity; by what has appeared,
hitherto, they have only raised our longing
to see their posthumous works.

'The author of "Doctae Rusticantis Liter-
atum Olim," is but a mere phraseologist,
the philological publisher is but a translator,
but I expected better usage from Mr. Abel
Roper who is an original.'

———

'. . . Ægri somnia.'—Hor., 'Ars. Poet.' v. 7.
A sick man's dream.

My correspondent who has acquired the
faculty of entering into other men's thoughts,
having in pursuance to a former letter sent
me an account of certain useful discoveries
he has made by the help of that invention,
I shall communicate the same to the public
in this paper.

'Mr. Ironside,—On the 11th day of October
in the year 1712, having left my body locked
up safe in my study, I repaired to the Grecian
Coffee-house, where, entering into the pineal

gland of a certain eminent Free-thinker, I
made directly to the highest part of it which
is the seat of the understanding, expecting
to find there a comprehensive knowledge of
all things human and divine, but to my no
small astonishment I found the place narrower
than ordinary, insomuch that there was not any
room for a miracle, prophecy, or separate spirit.

'This obliged me to descend a storey lower
into the imagination, which I found larger indeed, but cold and comfortless. I discovered
prejudice, in the figure of a woman standing
in a corner with her eyes close shut, and her
forefingers stuck in her ears, many words in a
confused order but spoken with great em-
phasis, issued from her mouth. These being
condensed by the coldness of the place, formed
a sort of mist through which methought I
saw a great castle with a fortification cast
round it and a tower adjoining to it that
through the windows appeared to be filled
with racks and halters. Beneath the castle I
could discern vast dungeons, and all about it
lay scattered the bones of men. It seemed to
be garrisoned by certain men in black of
gigantic size and most terrible forms. But
as I drew near, the terror of the appearance
vanished, and the castle I found to be only a
church whose steeple with its clock and bell-
ropes was mistaken for a tower filled with
racks and halters. The terrible giants in
black shrunk into a few innocent clergymen.

'The dungeons were turned into vaults designed only for the habitation of the dead, and the fortifications proved to be a churchyard with some scattered bones in it, and a plain stone wall round it.

'I had not been long here before my curiosity was raised by a loud noise that I heard in the inferior region. Descending thither, I found a mob of the Passions assembled in a riotous manner. Their tumultuary proceedings soon convinced me that they affected democracy. After much noise and wrangle they at length all hearkened to Vanity, who proposed the raising of a great army of notions, which she offered to lead against those dreadful phantoms in the imagination that had occasioned all this uproar.

'Away posted Vanity and I after her to the storehouse of ideas, where I beheld a great number of lifeless notions confusedly thrown together, but upon the approach of Vanity they began to crawl. Here were to be seen among other odd things, sleeping deities, corporeal spirits, and worlds formed by chance, with an endless variety of heathen notions, the most irregular and grotesque imaginable. And with these were jumbled several of Christian extraction, but such was the dress and light they were put in, and their features were so distorted, that they looked little better than heathens.

'There was likewise assembled no small

number of phantoms in strange habits, who proved to be idolatrous priests of different nations. Vanity gave the word, and straightway the Talapoins, Faquirs, Bramines, and Bonzes drew up in a body. The right wing consisted of ancient heathen notions, and the left of Christians naturalised. All these together for numbers, composed a very formidable army, but the precipitation of Vanity was so great, and such was their own inbred aversion to the tyranny of rules and discipline that they seemed rather a confused rabble than a regular army. I could nevertheless observe that they all agreed in a squinting look or cast of their eyes towards a certain person in a mask who was placed in the centre, and whom by sure signs and tokens I discovered to be Atheism.

'Vanity had no sooner led her forces into the Imagination, but she resolved on storming the castle and giving no quarter. They began the assault with a loud outcry and great confusion. I for my part made the best of my way and re-entered my own lodging.

'Some time after enquiring at a bookseller's for "A Discourse on Free-thinking" which had made some noise, I met with the representative of all those notions drawn up in the same confused order upon paper. Sage Nestor.—I am, your most obedient humble Servant,   Ulysses Cosmopolita."

'N.B.—I went round the table but could not find a wit or mathematician among them.

'I imagine the account here given may be useful in directing to the proper cure of a Free-thinker. In the first place it is plain his understanding wants to be opened and enlarged, and he should be taught the way to order and methodise his ideas, to which end the study of the mathematics may be useful. I am farther of opinion that, as his imagination is filled with amusements arising from prejudice, and the obscure or false lights in which he sees things, it will be necessary to bring him into good company and manner and internal principles by which that phenomenon was formed, I shall in my next give you an account of it. I am in the meantime, —Your most obedient humble Servant,

"Ulysses Cosmopolita."'

INDEX OF AUTHORS